BUSINESS BOOTCAMP

From Overwhelmed
to In Command

BUSINESS BOOTCAMP

*Field-Tested Strategies from a Military
Leader to Scale Your Business*

☆ ☆ ☆

ERIC MCCONATY

TGS

Published in the United States by Eric McConaty, Dumfries, Virginia.

First Edition: March 2025
ISBN: 979-8-9929920-9-0

For permissions requests, contact eric@tgscoaching.com.

DISCLAIMER: The information in this book is intended for educational and informational purposes only. The author is not a licensed attorney, financial advisor, or business consultant. Readers are encouraged to seek professional advice before making business decisions. The stories and examples are based on real experiences but may be altered for privacy or narrative effect.

Library of Congress Cataloging-in-Publication Data is available upon request.

☆ ☆ ☆

DEDICATION

To my wife, Tammy, and our two incredible children, Kai and Emi— You are my squad, my strength, and my home front. Through every firefight and every victory, your unconditional support has been my greatest mission success. This book is for you.

Author's Note:
WHY I WROTE THIS BOOK

Business isn't bootcamp, but damn if it doesn't feel like it.

I step off the bus, boots barely hitting the dirt, and I'm swarmed. Drill sergeants—three of them—barking orders in my face, each one louder than the last. "Drop and give me twenty!" "Move to the line, you're too slow!" Every order clashes, every choice I make is wrong before I can finish it. The clock's a tyrant—there's never enough time for anything. I'm just scrambling to stay upright. The pressure is unbearable.

That was my first taste of bootcamp. But it's not just a Soldier's story, it's the reality too many small business owners live every day. Replace the drill sergeants for demanding customers, needy employees, and a phone that won't stop ringing. Trade the impossible deadlines for a flood of emails, overdue invoices, and inventory that's always behind. You're not dodging barked orders, you're juggling a business that pulls you in every direction, leaving you wondering if you'll ever catch your breath.

I've been there, and I've conquered it. For years, I lived in two completely different professional worlds, simultaneously. Each one demanding a different kind of leadership. By day, I was a senior federal employee, crafting strategies, steering policy, and driving execution across entire organizations. It was big-picture command: success wasn't about sweat, but systems set for others to run.

By night (and weekends), I stepped into my other role as a senior Non-Commissioned Officer in the Army National Guard where leadership looked completely different. Here, I was responsible for executing someone else's plan with discipline, motivation, and precision, forging Soldiers into a unit that never faltered. In this world, success was about getting things done the right way, every time, without fail.

It didn't take long for me to recognize the stark contrast between these two environments, each with its own strengths, yet my unique vantage point revealed where systems fall apart. In the military, well-designed processes transformed individuals into a cohesive, high-performing unit. Yet, many units lacked the staff or time to fully leverage these systems, relying instead on the foundational frameworks crafted by senior federal leaders, like me.

In the federal world, my ascent to senior levels exposed the fissures: bureaucracy stifled strategy, and leaders—often years removed from hands-on execution—struggled to develop actionable plans. Senior officials spent more time perfecting strategy documents than understanding the practical steps to implement them, leaving the mission adrift in a sea of process over purpose.

One day, it hit me. What if I can combine these two worlds. I brought military grit—discipline, systems, execution—to my federal role, and federal vision—strategy, oversight—to my National Guard role. The shift was seismic. I wasn't working harder; I was leading smarter. Teams clicked, stress dropped, morale soared, and chaos bent to my will. I'd cracked the code.

If it worked in the government—where inefficiency's practically a medal—I knew these same principles could transform business owners dying to break free. That's exactly what I do today, I'm a business coach and strategist who helps pull business owners out of bootcamp hell. I help them build systems that scale, and ignite leadership that lasts, not through burnout but through mastery. I've taken clients from 18-hour ultra marathon workdays to 4-5 vacations a year with passion projects on the side. I've watched revenues explode 100x, and legacies rise from dreams to reality.

That's why I wrote Business Bootcamp: to hand you a proven, step-by-step playbook, forged in the fire of military discipline and strategic expertise to scale your business without losing your sanity or your soul. This book is field-tested and ready for you to deploy. If you're tired of scrambling and ready to lead with strength and purpose, this is your call to action. Step up, take command, and let's build something extraordinary.

CONTENTS

Blue Phase: Growth

Gold Phase: Scaling and Sustaining

☆☆☆

Introduction

Take command of your team—this book hands you the tools to build a legacy you'll lead with pride. It's not here to peddle unrealistic promises of overnight success. If you're a small team leader (2-20 employees) trapped in chaos, overwhelmed by managing your crew, or pushing harder with little team traction, you're in the right place. You're not alone.

Too many business owners launch with bold dreams and raw determination, rallying a handful of employees to grow. Then reality strikes—endless to-dos, team missteps, and suddenly you're charging through a barrage with no clear route to lead your squad. In the military, we call this the 'fog of war'—a blinding haze where every move teeters on uncertainty, every decision a risk. That's your business now: a battlefield cloaked in fog, pulling your team in every direction. Sound familiar? Perfect. You're exactly who this book targets.

Let me tell you something that might surprise you: hustling isn't the answer. If success were just about putting in more hours, every person grinding away at two jobs would be living on a private island.

Success hinges on doing the right things—strategically, decisively. And that starts with stepping back, taking a breath, and looking at your business with fresh eyes. If you're stuck doing it all, this book will show you how to delegate and build a business that runs without you drowning in the details. It's time to slice through the fog and lead like the commander your business demands.

Here's how we're going to do it. This book guides you through four phases—Foundation, Operations, Growth, Sustainability—united as FOGS, your battle-tested map to navigate the fog of war. In military bootcamp, phases are color-coded to track a recruit's rise from chaos: Red for the raw beginning, White for skill-building, Blue for advancement, Gold for mastery. FOGS follows that tradition, with each phase clearing a layer of fog, bringing clarity where chaos once ruled.

Red Phase- Foundation: Forge your vision, mission, mindset, and strategy—this sets the direction and purpose for you and your team. It's the first strike to clear the fog, uniting your squad under a shared goal.

White Phase- Operations: Once your foundation is solid, you need systems and processes to keep things running without chaos. This is how you free yourself and your team from the day-to-day grind and create consistency. Operations sharpen your focus, cutting deeper into the haze.

Blue Phase- Growth: Here's where momentum kicks in. Growth is about finding and reaching the right customers, building relationships, and scaling your business without losing your sanity.

Growth lights the way, showing you the path forward, scaling your team's efforts.

Gold Phase- Sustainability: This is the long game. It's about maintaining what you've built, handling growth responsibly, and making sure your business doesn't just survive—it thrives for years to come. Sustainability locks in your vision, ensuring the fog never returns.

What sets this book apart: you'll master principles to transform your business, backed by actionable AI tools woven into every phase of FOGS. At each chapter's end, you'll find targeted AI prompts—not just for brainstorming, but to analyze data, automate tasks, engage customers, and predict trends, helping you execute with precision. No fluff, no empty theories—just cutting-edge tools to deploy now and drive results.

The fog of war never truly goes away—but with the lessons in this book, you'll learn to see through it, adapt, and lead your business and team to victory.

Before we dive into the FOGS framework, let me take you back to where my leadership journey began—a dusty valley in Afghanistan, surrounded by chaos, where I learned the hard way that mindset is the first step to cutting through any fog. In Chapter 1, I'll share that story and show how the same clarity I found under fire applies to your squad's foundation. From there, we'll build through each FOGS phase—starting with your team's vision and mission, then sharpening operations, fueling growth, and locking in sustainability—so your business can thrive, no matter the battlefield.

Are you ready? Good. Fall in, let's march through the fog.

RED PHASE:
THE FOUNDATION OF YOUR BUSINESS

☆★☆

Chapter 1
MINDSET AND SELF

There I was, crouched in a dusty valley in Afghanistan, a place so remote it felt like the end of the earth, leading my squad through a storm of chaos. The kind of place where the silence could kill you, and when the noise started, you almost wished it was silent again. Gunfire erupted in every direction, a symphony of chaos with no conductor, as I directed my team to take cover. Mortars shook the ground beneath us, their concussive blasts ripping through the air, while rockets screamed overhead like they had a personal vendetta. The sharp crack of rifles echoed closer and closer, and my head was spinning, trying to make sense of it all for my squad—my ears ringing so loud I couldn't tell if the shots came from the mountains, the valley, or the corners of my own mind.

We were pinned down. No clear path out. The dust mixed with smoke, creating a haze so thick it felt like the entire world had narrowed down to this one valley, this one moment. I felt it—the weight of everything. My chest was tight, my breath shallow, and that sick, heavy feeling of helplessness started creeping in. I've been through some tough situations, but this one? This one felt like the universe had stacked the deck against us.

In the middle of the chaos, surrounded by dust and desperation, the thought hit me: *Why the hell did I join the Army?* It wasn't the first time I'd asked myself that, but it was the loudest. It wasn't just a passing thought—it was the kind of question that grips you by the collar and demands an answer.

The answer wasn't some grand, noble dream or burning desire to be a hero that got me here. The truth was simpler, and maybe a little raw. It wasn't about medals or glory; it was about finding purpose and a way out.

I grew up in a blue-collar town not far from D.C., where the world felt both close and impossibly far away. On September 11th, I watched the towers fall, and that hit home in ways I can't describe. We were just miles from the Pentagon, and the shockwaves weren't just figurative— they were literal. Fear, anger, and a need to do *something* rippled through my community.

But if I'm being honest, it wasn't just about 9/11. It was also about getting out. My hometown wasn't bad, but it was small. Ambition didn't stretch far, and college wasn't on the table for me. My SAT scores? Let's just say they were more of a warning sign than a badge of honor. The Army wasn't just an option—it was *the* option. My way out. My way to prove that I could be something more than what I felt the world expected of me.

So, there I was, crouched in the dirt, gunfire all around, asking myself *why*. And in that moment, it clicked. My "why" wasn't just a reason—it was my anchor. It reminded me that I wasn't here by accident. I'd chosen this path for a reason, even if it felt impossible at the moment. That clarity didn't make the bullets stop flying, but it made me stop panicking.

Instead of getting swallowed by the chaos, I started focusing. I remembered my training. I thought about what needed to happen next. The question shifted from *why the hell am I here* to *how do we get out of this alive?* I stopped thinking about the impossibility of the situation and started breaking it down. One step at a time. Where's the cover? Where's the team? What's the next move?

That mindset saved my squad that day. It turned chaos into clarity. It didn't matter that the situation felt impossible; what mattered was what I did next.

And this? This is exactly what you need in your business. You'll face situations that feel overwhelming, where everything's on fire, and it feels like the walls are closing in. The temptation will be to throw your hands up or fixate on everything going wrong. But here's the truth: Chaos will happen. Challenges are guaranteed. The question is, will you let them paralyze you, or will you focus on what you can control?

Your mindset is your greatest asset. It's what separates the people who stay stuck from the ones who move forward. If you're in the middle of your own firefight right now—whether it's finances, team issues, or just the grind of running a business—pause. Breathe. Remember why you're doing this. Then focus on the next move. Not ten steps ahead. Just the next one.

Business throws chaos at you—your mindset determines if it breaks you or builds you. Focus on what you can control, and the impossible becomes doable. One step at a time.

Understanding Your Team's Why

Alright, let's get to the heart of it all—your team's why. And no, I'm not talking about some inspirational quote you saw on Instagram or that feel-good poster hanging in your local coffee shop. I'm talking about the raw, real reason your team started this business together in the first place. Without a clear why, your squad is just swinging at problems blindly, hoping something eventually works. But when you and your team know your why—when you really know it—it becomes the engine driving everything. It's what keeps your crew moving when everything else feels like it's falling apart.

Think back to those moments when you've felt proud of what you're doing. Maybe it was the smile on a customer's face after they used your product or service. Maybe it was seeing the positive impact your business had on your community. Or maybe it was that quiet realization that you're building something bigger than yourself—something that matters. Those moments? That's your why in action. That's what you need to hold onto when the going gets tough.

But let's be honest here: if your answer to "what's my why" is "I want to make money" or "I want to be successful," then we've got a problem. That's not a why—that's the bare minimum. Everyone wants those things. To get to your real why, you need to dig deeper. You need to ask yourself the tough questions that most people are too afraid to face. Ready? Here we go:

- Ask your team, "why do we exist beyond profit?" Was it just a hobby we turned into a hustle, or is there something deeper driving us?

- What problem are we solving, and why does that problem matter to *us*? If it doesn't matter to us, it's not going to matter to anyone else.

- How do we want to impact our customers, our team, and our community? Because a business built only around you isn't going to last.

- What legacy do we want to leave? No pressure, but you're building something that could outlast all of you. What do you want that to look like?

When you can answer these questions without hesitation, you've just found the thing that's going to keep you grounded when everything feels like it's falling apart. That's not just a nice idea—it's the foundation of your business.

But here's the kicker: once you've nailed down your why, you can't just toss it on a sticky note and forget about it. Your why isn't a decoration—it's the lifeblood of your business. It should show up in everything you do. Your products, your services, your branding, your customer interactions—hell, even how you handle complaints. When your business aligns with your why, people notice. Customers see the authenticity. Employees feel the purpose. And that's what builds trust, loyalty, and long-term success.

Here's where it gets practical. When your business decisions align with your why, things start to make sense. You're not flailing, trying to figure out what to do next. You're moving forward with clarity and purpose, knowing exactly what you're aiming for. It becomes easier to say no to distractions, shiny objects, and opportunities that don't fit your mission. That's the power of keeping your why front and center—it's your compass, always pointing you in the right direction.

And this isn't just about you. A clear why is a strategic advantage. When your team understands it, they rally behind it. When your customers believe in it, they stick with you. And when your decisions come from that deeper purpose, your business becomes unstoppable.

Here's a sobering stat: 70% of small businesses fail within five years, often because they lack a clear direction. That's why your team's why isn't just feel-good fluff—it's the compass that keeps your squad from wandering into the fog of failure. Ask your crew: 'What problem are we solving together?' and build from there.

So, here's your mission: figure out your team's why. Make it the backbone of everything you do. Keep it visible, revisit it often, and let it guide every step of your journey. This isn't fluff. It's the foundation for building something that lasts—and something that matters.

Now get to work. Nail down your team's why and watch how everything else starts to fall into place. Your team will be more focused, more productive, and a hell of a lot less stressed when you're running a business built on purpose. Trust me, it's the best thing you'll ever do for yourself, your business, and the people you serve.

Mindset: The Only Thing That'll Keep You from Throwing in the Towel

Alright, now that you've nailed down your *why*, let's talk about something just as important—your mindset. And not just any mindset. I'm talking about the *growth mindset*. Yeah, I know, it might sound like one of those Instagram buzzwords slapped onto a picture of a mountain with a cheesy quote about "believing in yourself," but trust me, this is the real deal. A growth mindset is the difference between a business owner who thrives and one who ends up buried under burnout, wondering where it all went wrong.

Here's the truth: none of the principles in this book—vision, strategy, operations, scaling—are going to help your team if you don't have the right mindset as their leader. Without it, your squad will be stuck in a cycle of blame. The economy, the competition, your customers—hell, maybe even your dog will start taking the heat. But here's the hard truth: the only thing that's going to change your business is your leadership mindset. Your mindset is the fuel that keeps your crew's engine running when the road gets rough.

Let me paint you a picture. When I was in the Army, whining about a tough situation wasn't exactly an option. Sure, some days felt like the universe had it out for us—everything that could go wrong did, and then some. But we had a choice: adapt, improvise, and push through, or let the situation bury us. That's the same choice you have in your business. Challenges are going to hit, and they're going to hit hard. But a growth mindset keeps you grounded. It helps you shift from *Why is this happening to me?* to *What can I do about this? How do I move forward?*

The magic of a growth mindset is that it turns failure into a stepping stone instead of a dead end. Let's say your big marketing campaign tanks. You could throw your hands up and say, *nothing ever works!* Or you could take a step back and ask, *what can I learn from this? Was it my messaging? Did I target the wrong audience? What adjustments can I make for next time?* That's the difference. A fixed mindset sees failure as final; a growth mindset sees it as feedback.

And here's the kicker: success isn't going to happen overnight. It's not a straight line. It's a messy, unpredictable climb that tests your patience and resilience at every turn. If you expect smooth sailing, you're in for a rude awakening. But when you embrace the bumps, learn from every misstep, and keep going, you start to see those challenges for what they really are: opportunities to grow.

But let me be clear—a growth mindset isn't just about being tough. It's about being open. Open to learning, to adapting, and to changing the way you think and operate. If you're holding on to the idea that you already know it all, I hate to break it to you, but your business is already behind. The ones who thrive are the ones who stay curious, who look at setbacks and think, *How do I get better from here?*

This is where your *why* ties back in. Without it, keeping a growth mindset is next to impossible. Your why is what gives you the strength to keep going when things feel impossible. It's the reminder of what you're building and why it matters. When you're knee-deep in chaos, when the obstacles feel overwhelming, your why becomes your anchor. It keeps you grounded and focused on solutions, not just problems.

Here's the bottom line: if you want to build a business that lasts, you've got to embrace the growth mindset. Be ready to fail, but also be ready to learn, adapt, and improve. When you do, you'll create something strong enough to survive anything—and something you actually enjoy running. The chaos won't feel so overwhelming because you'll be the one in control.

So, if you're still with me, you're already on the right track. From here on out, we're going to dive into the strategies, systems, and actions that will transform your business. But remember: without the right mindset, none of it's going to stick. So, keep your head in the game, stay open to the process, and let's get to work. The hard part isn't over—but you've already proven you're ready for it.

☆★☆

Chapter 2:

VISION

Alright, let's set the stage. Imagine it's 2008, and the global economy is doing a slow-motion nosedive. Meanwhile, a private space company run by a guy who just cashed out of PayPal is busy blowing up rockets in the middle of nowhere, rallying his team to push boundaries. Sound promising? That guy, of course, is Elon Musk. Now, regardless of how you feel about his politics or his tweets, you can't deny one thing: the guy knows how to create and execute a vision with his squad. And with SpaceX, that vision wasn't just big—it was colossal. Colonizing Mars. Seriously, he wasn't talking about sending a couple of satellites into orbit or launching a fancy telescope. No, Musk set his squad's sights on building a multiplanetary civilization. A little ambitious, don't you think?

Here's the thing about a vision like that: it doesn't come with a neatly laid-out map. Back in the early days, SpaceX's rockets weren't known for their reliability. In fact, their first three launches ended in fiery disasters. They were hemorrhaging money, their critics were laughing, and even Musk himself admitted they were a failed launch away from bankruptcy. But what kept them moving forward? The vision. That laser-focused, audacious dream of making life multiplanetary.

When you have a vision that big, it forces you to think differently. Instead of just trying to make rockets that work, SpaceX was driven to make rockets that could land themselves—something no one had done before. Why? Because reusability was the key to making space travel affordable. And affordability was the key to putting a human on Mars. Every decision they made—no matter how small—aligned with that ultimate goal. It wasn't about winning in the short term. It was about playing the long game.

Now, here's the part where the vision really shows its power: SpaceX stuck to it even when everything seemed stacked against them. After those three failed launches, they could've packed it in, taken the loss, and moved on. But they didn't. They took every failure as a lesson, stayed focused, and finally nailed it on the fourth launch. That one successful flight? It saved the company. Today, they're launching more rockets than anyone else, landing boosters on ships in the middle of the ocean and building the kind of tech that can actually take people to Mars.

So, what's the takeaway for you? A strong vision isn't just about dreaming big. It's about giving yourself and your team a north star—a direction that keeps you moving forward, even when the path gets rocky. A good vision pushes you to think strategically, adapt creatively, and stay resilient in the face of setbacks.

You don't have to be building rockets to Mars for this to matter. Whether your business is a bakery, a consulting firm, or a tech startup, your vision is what drives everything. It's what turns setbacks into stepping stones and keeps you going when the world feels like it's on fire. And if SpaceX can go from fiery failures to redefining space travel, imagine what you can do with a clear, focused vision for your business.

Alright, now that we've launched this chapter, let's figure out how to craft a vision that's bold, practical, and built to get you where you want to go. Because unlike SpaceX's first three launches, we're aiming to stick the landing on the first try.

So, what makes a good vision?

First, your team's vision needs to be specific. We're not here to dream about 'changing the world' or 'becoming rich'—we're talking about concrete, actionable goals. Your squad's vision should answer questions like: What problem are we solving together? Who are we serving as a team? and Why does it matter to us?

Second, a good vision needs to be *inspiring*. It's not just a business goal—it's a mission that lights a fire under you and keeps you going when the going gets tough. When the world is throwing curveballs at you, you should be able to pull out your vision like a secret weapon. It should be something that gets you out of bed at 5 a.m., ready to conquer the day—even when you'd rather hit snooze and pretend it's Saturday.

Lastly, your vision should be *achievable*, but not so easy that it doesn't make you stretch. It should challenge you. If you've set a goal that's too simple, you're not pushing yourself enough. On the flip side, don't make it so unrealistic that you feel like you're chasing a unicorn across a rainbow. Be realistic but challenge yourself to get there. Balance ambition with a solid understanding of what can actually be done.

Here's the proof: 80% of teams with a shared vision outperform those without, according to studies of collaborative workplaces. Your squad's vision—specific, actionable, and collective—sets you apart from the 20% floundering in ambiguity. Start by asking: 'What are we building together?

Now, how do you create it?

Here's the thing—creating a vision isn't some abstract art project where you slap together a bunch of motivational quotes, throw in a few Pinterest-worthy images, and call it a day. It's not about 'manifesting' success or crafting something that looks good on a poster. It's strategic work. It's gathering your squad, shutting out the noise, and really thinking about the future of your business together. So, if you're ready to get serious, here's how to get started:

Step 1: Start with the problem you're solving.

The best businesses solve real, tangible problems. So, what's your business solving? Get specific. Don't just say, "I want to help people." *Who* are you helping, and *how*? The clearer you get on this, the easier it'll be to build your vision around it. Remember, if you're not solving a meaningful problem, you're just adding noise to an already crowded world.

Step 2: Identify your long-term goal.

Where do you want your business and your team to be in 5, 10, or even 15 years? Don't be afraid to think big—dreams are free, after all. But dreaming big without a plan? That's just wishful thinking. Your long-term goal needs to be ambitious enough to inspire you but realistic enough that you can break it down into actionable steps. Think of it as the North Star for your business—distant but always guiding you.

Step 3: Tap into your values.

Why are you doing this in the first place? What's the deeper motivation that gets you out of bed on the hard days? Maybe you're driven by a desire to make a difference, to achieve financial freedom, or to prove the doubters wrong. Whatever your motivation, your vision has to align with your core values. If it doesn't, you'll find yourself running out of steam the moment things get tough. A vision without values is just a hollow goal—it might look nice, but it won't keep you going when the grind gets real.

Step 4: Keep it simple.

It's tempting to get all philosophical and complex with your vision—adding layers of meaning and metaphors that sound impressive but don't actually mean anything. Resist the urge. A good vision is simple, clear, and easy to remember. If you can't explain it in one sentence, it's probably too complicated. Your vision should inspire action, not confusion.

That's it. Four straightforward steps to creating a vision that's rooted in purpose, built on strategy, and strong enough to guide you through whatever challenges come your way. Don't overthink it—just start. Because the sooner you clarify your vision, the sooner you can start building the business you've been dreaming of.

Avoiding Common Pitfalls

Now, before you dive headfirst into crafting your vision, let's talk about the traps that trip up so many business owners. Because let's be real, creating a vision sounds straightforward until you find yourself overcomplicating it, chasing shiny objects, or letting your ego hijack the process. To keep you on track, here are the most common pitfalls to watch out for—and how to avoid them:

1. Making it too vague.

"I want to be successful" or "I want to help people" might sound nice, but let's face it—those are fluff. If your vision is too broad or generic, it won't inspire you or guide your decisions. A good vision has clarity and focus. It's specific enough to give you direction but flexible enough to adapt as your business evolves.

2. Overcomplicating it.

Some people think a vision needs to be this grand, poetic statement worthy of being carved in stone. It doesn't. If your vision is so complex you can't remember it without checking your notes, it's not doing its job. Keep it simple, clear, and actionable.

3. Chasing trends instead of staying true to your values.

It's easy to get caught up in what's "hot" right now, whether it's the latest business buzzwords or whatever your competitors are doing. But if your vision doesn't align with your core values, it's not going to stick. Trends come and go—your vision needs to be grounded in what truly matters to you.

4. Failing to communicate it.

A vision is useless if it stays locked in your head. Your team needs to understand it, your customers need to feel it, and your decisions need to reflect it. If no one knows what your vision is, you might as well not have one.

5. Letting it collect dust.

Writing down your vision and then shoving it in a drawer is a recipe for failure. Your vision isn't a one-and-done exercise—it's a living, breathing part of your business. Revisit it regularly, adjust it as needed, and make sure it's woven into everything you do.

The good news? These pitfalls are easy to dodge if you stay intentional and keep your focus on what truly matters. Now that you know what to avoid, you're ready to create a vision that not only inspires but drives real results. Let's make sure your vision works as hard as you

Final Thoughts

So, here's the bottom line: your vision is the compass that guides your business through the chaos. It's not just a nice idea or a feel-good exercise—it's the foundation for every decision you'll make, every challenge you'll face, and every win you'll celebrate. Without it, you're just wandering aimlessly, hoping to stumble across success. But with it? You've got a clear direction, a purpose that keeps you grounded, and a reason to keep going when the road gets tough.

Crafting a vision isn't about perfection—it's about clarity. It's about knowing what you're building, why it matters, and how it aligns with your values. And once you have that vision, it's not something you write down and forget about. It's something you live, breathe, and embed into every part of your business.

Take the time to create a vision that excites you, motivates your team, and resonates with your customers. Make it the driving force behind everything you do. Because when your vision is clear, your path becomes clearer too.

You've got this. Now, let's take that vision and start turning it into reality.

Let's Put This into Action

A.I. can sharpen your Foundation even further. Tools like ChatGPT or market analysis platforms (e.g., IBM Watson) can scan industry trends, customer reviews, and competitor data to reveal gaps you might miss. For example, a bakery owner might prompt A.I. with: 'Analyze bakery trends in my city—what are customers craving most?' The A.I. might uncover a rising demand for gluten-free options, helping you craft a vision that's ahead of the curve. Use the A.I. prompts at the end of this chapter to dig into your market and align your strategy with real-time insights.

Here's the fun part—putting technology to work for you. If you've never used A.I. tools like GPTs before, don't worry. Think of it like having a brainstorming partner that never gets tired, doesn't judge your ideas, and is always ready to help you tackle a problem. This book includes prompts at the end of many chapters to help you take immediate action on what you've just learned.

Let me break down how to use this first prompt:

1. **Pick your A.I. tool.**

There are plenty of A.I. platforms out there, and GPT models (like ChatGPT) are some of the best for creative problem-solving, generating ideas, and organizing your thoughts. If you're new, start with a tool like ChatGPT, which is intuitive and user-friendly.

2. **Open the tool and start the conversation.**

Once you're in, you'll see a text box—this is where the magic happens. Simply type or paste the prompt into the box. Think of it like giving you're A.I. assistant clear instructions.

3. **Be specific.**

The more context you give the A.I., the better the response will be. If you're asking it to help craft a vision for your business, include details like what your business does, who you serve, and what your long-term goals are. For example, instead of just saying, "Help me write a vision," you might say, "Help me write a vision for my small landscaping business that focuses on eco-friendly solutions and sustainable practices."

4. **Iterate.**

Don't settle for the first response. If it's not quite what you're looking for, refine the input. You can say things like, "Make it shorter," "Focus more on innovation," or "Give me examples tailored to small businesses." A.I. tools are designed to collaborate with you, so treat it as a back-and-forth conversation.

5. **Use the response as a starting point.**

Remember, A.I. isn't a magic wand that creates perfection on the first try. It's a tool to help you think more clearly and organize your ideas. Take what it gives you, tweak it, and make it your own.

Now, here's your first prompt to use:

'What are the top trends in [your industry] in [your city] over the past year?' Use the insights to refine your vision and strategy, ensuring your Foundation aligns with customer demand.

Follow on Prompt:

"Help me create a clear and concise vision statement for my business. The business is focused on [insert your industry or niche], and I want the vision to reflect [insert what matters to you most, e.g., solving a particular problem, empowering a community, creating something innovative]. My long-term goal is to [insert your ultimate goal, e.g., grow into a sustainable company, impact lives, create jobs, or expand into new markets]. Make sure the vision is specific, inspiring, and aligned with my values, which include [insert your core values like integrity, growth, impact, etc.]. Keep it simple, easy to remember, and powerful enough to motivate me and my team every day."

☆★☆

Chapter 3:
MISSION

L et me tell you about a time I worked with a client who led a struggling Mexican restaurant, managing a small team of 10. You've probably been to a place like this: good food, decent prices, but nothing really stood out. The kind of restaurant that was just there. No identity. No purpose. His crew was grinding day in and day out, hoping sheer effort would translate into success. Spoiler alert—it didn't

When the owner came to me, he was frustrated. Business wasn't terrible, but it wasn't great either. He felt stuck. Customers came and went, but they weren't coming back as regulars. The team was working hard—really hard—but they weren't moving the needle. It was like trying to fill a bucket with a hole in the bottom. They had no direction, no focus. Just a lot of effort poured into a lot of nothing.

We started with a deep dive into what they were actually trying to accomplish. I asked the owner, "What's your mission? Why does your restaurant exist?" And, let me tell you, the look on his face was priceless—like I'd just asked him to solve a quantum physics equation. He rattled off generic answers like "to make great food" or "to serve the community." And while those were nice thoughts, they weren't actionable. They didn't set the restaurant apart or give the team something to rally around.

So, we got to work. We stripped it all back, starting with the food. What was unique about the restaurant? What was the one thing they could deliver better than anyone else? It turns out the owner's grandmother had passed down a killer recipe for mole sauce. It was rich, complex, and a little spicy—the kind of sauce you'd remember long after the meal. I asked him why it wasn't the centerpiece of the menu. His answer? "I guess I never thought about it like that." Bingo.

That mole sauce became the heart of the restaurant. We restructured the menu around it, featuring signature dishes that highlighted the sauce. But we didn't stop there. We rewrote the mission to reflect this newfound focus: *To bring the bold, authentic flavors of my grandmother's kitchen to every table.* Suddenly, the restaurant wasn't just a place to eat—it had a story. A purpose. And, most importantly, a mission that guided every decision.

We trained the staff to tell that story to every customer. From the moment people walked in, they were immersed in the restaurant's mission. The decor was updated to reflect the heritage and boldness of the food. Marketing became laser-focused on the idea of authenticity and flavor, with the mole sauce taking center stage. It wasn't just a restaurant anymore—it was an experience.

And here's the thing: everything changed. Customers weren't just ordering food—they were buying into a story, a mission. Word spread. Regulars started coming back, bringing friends and family to "try the mole sauce they'd been raving about." Revenue shot up. The team, once aimless and burned out, now worked with purpose and pride. Every decision—from which dishes to add to the menu, to how to market events—was filtered through the lens of that mission.

That's the power of a clear mission. It turns a business from a wandering ship into one with a clear destination. It aligns your team, attracts your customers, and gives you a guiding star for every decision. Without it, you're just treading water, hoping something sticks. But with it? You're unstoppable.

So, what's your mission? What's the reason your business exists? If you don't have an answer, it's time to find one. Because when you do, you won't just be running a business—you'll be leading a movement.

So, what makes a good mission?

Now that we've hammered home why a clear mission is critical, let's talk about what makes a mission statement actually *work*—and, just as importantly, how to create one that doesn't leave your team, or you, wondering what it's supposed to mean.

First things first: a mission statement isn't a fluffy slogan designed to make your business sound fancy. It should be clear, direct, and grounded in what your team actually does together and why it matters. No manifestos. No corporate jargon. The goal is simple: create a mission statement with your squad that's easy to understand and actionable.

Here's what it needs to answer:

- **What do you do?**

- **Why do you do it?**

- **How do you do it?**

Think of it like this: If your vision is the dream, your mission is the battle plan. It's the day-to-day grind that gets you closer to the bigger picture. Without a clear mission, all that hustle? It's just spinning your wheels. You're busy, but you're not moving forward.

Take this as an example: Imagine your business provides clean water to rural communities. A mission like, "We provide sustainable, clean water solutions to underserved areas through innovative technology and community-driven efforts," works because it's clear and to the point. It tells you what the business does, who it helps, and how it does it—no fluff, no guessing.

Consider this: 60% of small businesses operate without a written mission, leaving their teams directionless. Your squad's mission—clear, actionable, and team-crafted—puts you ahead of that majority, giving your crew a rallying cry to follow.

So, how do you create a mission statement that works with your team?

Here's the breakdown:

1. Get to the point.

Skip the fluff. This isn't the time to write poetry about your aspirations. Your mission statement should give your team and your customers a clear picture of what your business does and why it exists.

2. Focus on your values.

What do you stand for? If integrity, sustainability, or innovation drive your business, make sure your mission reflects that. A strong mission should connect to your team's core values and remind you— and everyone else—why you're in this game beyond just making a profit.

3. Be specific, but not overcomplicated.

"To sell products" or "To be the best" is way too vague. But something like, "To help small businesses scale their operations through affordable and efficient tech solutions," gives direction without overloading the brain. It's clear, actionable, and focused.

4. Highlight your unique strengths.

What sets you apart? Maybe it's your stellar customer service, an innovative product, or a pricing model no one can beat. Your mission should show what makes your business stand out in the crowd.

5. Keep it actionable.

A mission statement isn't just wall art or a website decoration. It's a filter for every decision you make. When a new opportunity comes along, your mission should help you decide: Does this align with our purpose, or is it just a shiny distraction?

Once you've nailed your mission, don't let it collect dust. Share it with your team, embed it into your business culture, and let it guide your strategy. A good mission isn't just a statement—it's a blueprint. It keeps you focused, aligned, and intentional, helping you avoid the chaos that comes from doing too much with no clear direction.

Your mission is more than words. It's a promise to yourself, your team, and your customers about what you're building and why it matters. Get it right, and it'll become one of your most valuable tools for success.

Common Pitfalls to Avoid

Now, before you go running off to craft your perfect mission statement, let's talk about the pitfalls. Because, trust me, you don't want to end up with a half-baked mission that's as useful as a screen door on a submarine.

Here's the thing: Writing a mission statement seems like a no-brainer, but it's easy to fall into the trap of making it too vague, too broad, or worse—completely irrelevant to your business's real purpose. So, let's break down the most common mistakes people make when creating a mission statement, so you can avoid them and get it right the first time. No one wants to be stuck trying to dig themselves out of a hole, especially when it could have been avoided with a little foresight.

So, buckle up—these are the mission statement mistakes you don't want to make.

1. Being Too Vague

You've seen them: those mission statements that sound like they were written by a robot trying to be motivational. You know, the "We aim to make a positive impact on the world" kind of fluff. That's nice and all, but it doesn't tell anyone what you *actually do*. Think about it—if you have a vague mission, your team doesn't know what direction to head in, and your customers won't know what to expect. It's like being handed a map with no destination. Make it specific—what exactly are you trying to achieve?

2. Focusing Only on Profits

Look, I get it, money is important. You wouldn't be in business if you didn't want to make some cash. But if your mission is all about the greenbacks, you're missing the bigger picture. You're not just running a business to line your pockets—you're providing value, solving problems, and making an impact. If your mission is strictly about profit, your customers, employees, and even your own motivation will be dry as a desert. Build a mission that inspires—not just for the short-term win, but for the long haul.

3. Lack of Clarity

A mission statement should be as clear as your grandma's favorite recipe. It's not the place for fancy jargon, corporate speak, or overused buzzwords. If no one understands what your mission is saying, it's useless. Be direct. Think about the problems you solve, who you solve them for, and why it matters. You should be able to say your mission in one sentence without sounding like you're trying to sell a used car.

4. Overpromising

Sure, you want to be ambitious. But if your mission statement promises the moon and stars, you're setting yourself up for a hard fall. If you can't deliver on the big, lofty promises you're making, your customers and team will lose faith faster than you can say "back to the drawing board." Aim high, but keep your feet on the ground with realistic goals that you can actually achieve. The last thing you need is to be known for making promises you can't keep.

5. Not Revisiting It Regularly

You can't write a mission statement and then forget about it. This isn't a tattoo you get at 18 and never think about again. Your business evolves, your market shifts, and your goals change. Your mission should evolve with it. If your mission statement isn't being revisited and adjusted regularly, it's like trying to drive a car without ever checking the oil. Eventually, things are going to break down, and your business will stall.

Final Thoughts

Your mission isn't just a catchy phrase to slap on your website or throw into a meeting. It's the backbone of your business—the steady guide that keeps you focused, aligned, and moving in the right direction. A well-crafted mission simplifies decisions, rallies your team, and makes it crystal clear what you're here to do and why it matters.

When you take the time to define a mission that's clear, actionable, and rooted in your values, you're not just setting the stage for success— you're building the foundation for a business that stands out and stays strong, no matter what challenges come your way.

Keep it simple. Keep it meaningful. And most importantly, use it. A mission that isn't lived and breathed every day isn't a mission—it's just empty words. Let your mission be the driver that powers your business forward.

Let's Put This Into Action

This will help you craft a clear, no-nonsense mission statement that aligns with your business's true purpose and keeps everyone focused on what really matters. Paste this into you're A.I. tool of choice.

"Help me craft a straightforward and clear mission statement for my business. My goal is to clearly define what my business does, why it matters, and how we add value for our customers. I want to avoid vague language and over-promising. Keep it specific and realistic, focusing on the problem we're solving, who we're solving it for, and why it matters to our team and customers. Here's some information about my business:

- What we do: [Insert your business's primary function, e.g., we design and sell innovative fitness equipment].

- Who we serve: [Insert your target audience, e.g., busy professionals seeking to stay healthy].

- Why we exist: [Insert your purpose, e.g., to empower people to achieve their health goals efficiently].

Please help me craft a concise, inspiring mission statement that aligns with these details and includes our purpose, audience, and key actions."

☆★☆

Chapter 4:
STRATEGY

Alright, now that we've gotten your mission straightened out, let's talk about strategy. Let me take you back to my days as a federal employee. Like any government role, there were moments of monotony, sure—but then there were moments of pure chaos, where everything seemed to be falling apart. One of those moments hit when I took over an organization that was, to put it kindly, in disarray. The turnover rate in our subordinate units was sky-high, and policy violations were popping up faster than we could track them. It was the kind of situation that makes you wonder, "Why did I ever think this job was a good idea?"

At first, it was tempting to blame the people. After all, they were the ones making the mistakes and walking out the door. But the deeper I looked, the more I realized the real issue wasn't with the individuals—it was with the system they were working in. There was no strategy, no guidance, no foundation for success. People didn't know what was expected of them, so they made mistakes. And because they didn't feel like they were part of something meaningful, they left. It wasn't laziness; it was a complete lack of direction and purpose.

I knew we couldn't keep running this way. The mistakes were creating ripple effects, costing time, resources, and credibility. And the turnover? It was a revolving door of talent loss, leaving the team perpetually understaffed and overwhelmed. Something had to change.

That's when I realized we didn't just need quick fixes—we needed a strategy. A real, actionable plan to tackle both problems at the root. I gathered my team, and we started by laying everything out on the table: the mistakes, the exits, and the underlying issues. The picture that emerged was crystal clear—people weren't set up to succeed. Without proper training or clear expectations, they were flying blind. And when you fly blind, you crash.

Our strategy was simple but ambitious: we would create a professional training curriculum for all subordinate units. This wasn't going to be some cookie-cutter program slapped together to check a box. It had to be meaningful, practical, and, most importantly, tailored to our specific needs. We wanted every individual to leave the training not only with the skills to do their job but also with a clear sense of purpose and an understanding of how their role fit into the bigger picture.

But there was one big hurdle: funding. Training costs money, and we didn't have a spare dollar to throw around. So, we pitched the idea to our higher headquarters. We didn't just ask for money—we made the case that this training wasn't just for us. It was an investment in the entire organization, one that would pay dividends in improved performance, reduced turnover, and fewer mistakes. And you know what? They bought in. We got the funding we needed to make it happen.

Once we had the resources, my team went all in. They designed a curriculum that was engaging, straightforward, and action-oriented. It didn't just teach the basics—it set clear expectations, laid out responsibilities, and gave people the tools to succeed. And when we rolled it out, the impact was immediate. Turnover dropped. Mistakes became rare. People weren't just doing their jobs; they were doing them well, with confidence and purpose.

And here's the cherry on top: other departments started taking notice. They saw our results and wanted in. Our training became the gold standard, adopted across the organization as a model for success. What started as a way to fix a broken system turned into a blueprint for building something sustainable and scalable.

That's the power of strategy. Strategy isn't guesswork—it's a deliberate plan to tackle the root of your problems. Without a strategy, problems pile up—ours gave us a way to dig out and move forward.

So, if you're staring down your own set of challenges, ask yourself: Do you have a strategy, or are you just reacting to the chaos? Because if you want results, it starts with a plan.

So, what makes a good strategy?

Here's the deal—your strategy needs to have a clear vision. You can't just throw spaghetti at the wall and see what sticks. You need to know where you're going and why. If you're making decisions without a purpose or a target, you might as well be blindfolded, spinning in circles, and hoping you bump into success. A good strategy gives you that clarity. It tells you *what* you're trying to achieve and *how* you're going to get there. Without that direction, you're just flailing.

But, just like in the military (or any tough environment), you can't have a strategy without considering the terrain. And I'm not talking about physical terrain, I mean the environment your business is in. What are the external challenges? What does your competition look like? What's the market demand? A good strategy doesn't ignore the factors that affect your business. If you fail to take the terrain into account, you'll be caught off guard, just like we were when we didn't have a clear mission in the field. So yeah, get familiar with the battlefield, folks. Know what's coming at you.

Another key element of a solid strategy is a well-defined set of goals. But here's the kicker: the goals should be specific, measurable, and realistic. You can't aim for the moon unless you have a spaceship to get there. And if your goals are too vague, you're setting yourself up for failure. "Get more customers" is a terrible goal. "Increase customer acquisition by 25% over the next 6 months" is a much better one. It's clear, it's actionable, and it has a deadline. A good strategy isn't about wishful thinking; it's about concrete, measurable steps that you can actually achieve.

Let's talk about prioritization. Strategy isn't about doing everything at once—remember, we're not setting up campfires and building lookout towers here. A good strategy helps you focus on the most important things. It forces you to make tough calls, saying "No" to some opportunities so you can focus on the ones that matter. In the military, we don't just take every mission that comes our way. We prioritize based on what's going to move us toward the larger goal. In business, you need to do the same. Focus on your most impactful tasks, and say "No" to distractions.

Finally, a good strategy includes a system for adapting to changes. Nothing stays the same forever. The market shifts, customer needs change, and the unexpected always seems to pop up. Your strategy needs to be flexible enough to adapt while staying grounded in your core purpose. If you're rigid, you'll break when things go sideways. A good strategy is one that can take a hit, bounce back, and keep moving forward. Flexibility is key.

So, in short, a good strategy is a game plan that provides clarity, takes into account the external environment, sets clear and achievable goals, helps you prioritize, and includes flexibility for the unexpected. It's not about working harder; it's about working smarter, with a clear path toward your vision. And let's be real—it's better than just running around like a chicken with your head cut off, hoping something sticks. So if you want your business to thrive, get your strategy together—and stick to it. It's time to stop wandering aimlessly and start leading with purpose.

How do you create a strategy?

Now that we've covered what makes a good strategy, let's talk about how to actually create one. Because let's be real: knowing the theory is great, but it won't get you anywhere unless you take action. It's like knowing you should hit the gym but spending all afternoon binge-watching TV instead. Good intentions only get you so far—you need a game plan.

Step 1: Map Your Terrain.

The first step is to map your terrain. Just like I assessed the disarray in that federal organization, you need to look at your business landscape—your team's strengths, your market's demands, and the obstacles you're facing. Grab a notebook or open a spreadsheet with your squad, and list out what's working, what's breaking, and what's missing. In the Army, we conduct After Action Reviews and debriefs to spot patterns. For example, if your team of 2-10 is drowning in customer inquiries, that's a signal to prioritize communication systems.

Step 2: Define your vision and Set Objectives.

Your strategy needs a clear destination. If you've already done the work on your why, then you've got the foundation in place. Now it's time to zoom out and think big—what do you want your business to become? This is your North Star, the thing that drives every decision. Without a clear vision, you're just wandering aimlessly, hoping to stumble onto success. We created a strong vision in chapter 2, so the next part is to set your objectives. These should be specific, measurable, and tied to your mission from Chapter 3. Instead of a vague "grow sales," aim for "increase revenue by 15% in six months by targeting new local clients." Break it into milestones—maybe a 5% bump in three months—to keep your team motivated and on track.

Step 3: Break the vision into action plans.

A vision without action is just wishful thinking. Break your big-picture vision into smaller, actionable steps. Before moving forward use A.I. to analyze your data to spot key opportunities. You can use a prompt like *"Analyze trends for [your industry] in [your region] over 12 months."* For a coffee shop owner with a 4-person team A.I. revealed a 15% rise in demand for plant-based milk which guided their strategy. Once you identify the opportunity you need to set priorities. Ask yourself:

- What do I need to achieve in the next 6 months?

- What about the next year?

Set specific, measurable goals—none of that vague, half-hearted "I want to grow my business" nonsense. Be detailed. For example, that same coffee shop might have a priority to "expand the menu with plant-based options, train staff on new recipes, and target eco-conscious customers." Which aligned with their overall goal to increase revenue by 20% through new menu items." Measurable goals give you benchmarks to hit and keep you on track.

Step 4: Assess your resources and capacity.

Take inventory of what you've got and what you're missing. Do you have the tools, people, and budget to make your goals a reality? If not, figure out how to fill those gaps.

- Need more hands on deck? Maybe it's time to hire.

- Are your systems outdated? Look at investing in better tech.

- Short on cash? Focus on improving your cash flow or finding funding options.

A strategy without resources is like trying to drive cross-country on an empty tank—you're not getting far.

Step 5: Prioritize your efforts.

This is where most people get tripped up. You can't do everything at once. Trust me, I've tried, and all it leads to is burnout and chaos. Take a hard look at your goals and ask:

- What's going to have the biggest impact?

- What's most urgent?

Focus on the tasks that will give you the most bang for your buck. Knock out those high-priority items first and leave the distractions behind.

Step 6: Build in flexibility.

Even the best-laid plans will need adjustments. Markets shift, customer needs change, and competitors adapt. A good strategy isn't set in stone—it's a living, breathing roadmap that evolves with the times. Be open to pivoting when necessary but stay grounded in your vision. Flexibility doesn't mean abandoning your plan; it means being smart enough to adapt and keep moving forward.

Step 7: Communicate your strategy clearly.

This one's critical. Your strategy is useless if your team doesn't know what it is. Don't assume everyone's on the same page just because you mentioned it once in passing. Spell it out. Make sure your team knows:

- **What** the strategy is.

- **Why** it matters.

- **How** their work contributes to the bigger picture.

When your team understands the strategy and how they fit into it, they'll move with purpose and focus.

Step 8: Take action and evaluate progress.

A strategy is only as good as the execution. Once you've got the plan in place, start working on it immediately. Check in regularly to measure progress, evaluate what's working, and tweak the strategy as needed. Don't just set it and forget it—keep it active, relevant, and aligned with your goals.

With these steps, you're not just throwing spaghetti at the wall and hoping something sticks. You're creating a clear roadmap to move your business forward. And remember, strategies aren't perfect. They're designed to evolve and grow with your business. What matters is that you start now and stay committed to the process.

It's time to roll up your sleeves, get focused, and put your strategy into action. With the right plan in place, you'll stop spinning your wheels and start driving your business toward real, sustainable success. Let's go make it happen.

Avoiding Common Pitfalls

Now that you've got the blueprint for crafting a solid strategy, let's pump the brakes and talk about the landmines that can blow it all up. Even the best strategy can fall apart if you hit these common pitfalls. Avoid them, and you'll stay on track. Ignore them, and you're setting yourself up for a crash. Let's break it down:

1. Being Vague

If your strategy sounds like a fortune cookie—"Grow the business" or "Increase sales"—you're in trouble. A good strategy is specific. Spell out what needs to be done, by whom, and by when. Vague plans lead to wasted time and frustration. You wouldn't walk into a battlefield without a map, so don't head into business without clear directions.

2. Skipping Team Input

Thinking you can plan everything in a vacuum? Think again. Your team needs to buy in, and that starts with listening to them. Their insights can save you from blind spots. A strategy nobody supports is just wishful thinking. Make sure they're equipped and aligned to execute the plan effectively.

3. Refusing to Adapt

The world changes fast, and so should your strategy. If you're rigid and refuse to adjust, you'll get left behind. Stay flexible, monitor progress, and tweak your plan as needed. A strategy should evolve—it's a living document, not a relic.

4. Overlooking the Basics

Don't skip the fundamentals. Clear priorities, defined roles, and simple processes often get overlooked in favor of flashy tactics. But without a strong foundation, even the most ambitious strategy will crumble. Nail the basics before you start adding complexity.

5. Trying to Do Everything

A strategy that tackles too many objectives at once is a recipe for burnout and failure. Focus on the priorities that will make the biggest impact. Juggling too much will leave you with a mess and nothing to show for it.

6. Failing to Hold Accountability

A strategy is useless if no one—including you—is held accountable for executing it. Check in regularly, track progress, and make adjustments as needed. Don't let your strategy become a set-it-and-forget-it document. Stay on top of it, and keep your team aligned.

By steering clear of these pitfalls, you'll give your strategy a real chance to succeed. A good plan doesn't just sit on paper—it's something you actively work on, refine, and bring to life. Stay clear, stay focused, and keep moving forward.

Final Thoughts

Here's the bottom line: a solid strategy isn't just a nice-to-have—it's the engine that powers your business forward. It gives you clarity, direction, and a framework for making decisions that matter. Without it, you're just busy for the sake of being busy, running in circles and hoping for the best.

A well-crafted strategy ensures your efforts aren't wasted. It aligns your vision with actionable goals, uses your resources wisely, and keeps you focused on what truly moves the needle. Most importantly, it keeps you adaptable in the face of change and ready to tackle whatever challenges come your way.

Take the time to create a strategy that's clear, specific, and grounded in your mission. Communicate it, revisit it, and refine it as you go. When you do, you'll find yourself leading with purpose instead of reacting to chaos. And that's when real progress happens.

Now, it's time to take everything you've learned and start building a strategy that works. Because the sooner you start, the sooner you'll stop spinning your wheels and start driving toward the success you've been working so hard for. Let's make it happen.

Let's Put This Into Action

Use this A.I. prompt to help you create a solid strategy for your business:

"Help me create a strategy for my business. My vision is [insert vision], and my goals are [insert goals]. Identify 2–3 key focus areas that will help me close the gap between where I am and where I want to be. Break these focus areas down into actionable steps, and provide measurable metrics to track progress."

Bonus

I get it—these last few chapters can feel overwhelming. If your head's spinning right now, wondering where to even start, you're not alone. That's why I created something to help.

The **Strategic Planning Cheat Sheet** is a simple tool designed to cut through the noise and give you a clear, actionable plan. It's the exact document I use with my clients—the same framework that's helped small businesses 10X their revenue just by having a strategy in place.

Head over to my website https://tgscoaching.com/resources/ and download your copy today for free. I know you're really going to love it because it's so simple to use—and it really works.

Not in the mood to type? No problem—just scan the QR code below, and it's yours.

Let's take the guesswork out of strategy and get your business moving forward. You've got this.

WHITE PHASE: OPERATIONS

☆★☆

Chapter 5:

UNDERSTANDING THE ROLES IN YOUR BUSINESS

I was working with a client, let's call him Mike, who had just launched his own small IT consultancy. Mike was *all in*. He was hustling hard, wearing a million hats, and somehow, convinced that he was doing everything right. He was in the trenches every day—responding to emails, fixing technical problems, managing his team, trying to bring in new clients, and keeping track of finances. The man was running in circles, looking like a headless chicken with a laptop in hand. If you've ever tried to juggle too many things at once, you know exactly what I'm talking about.

One day, Mike hit a wall. He called me up, sounding like he was about to implode. "Eric, I can't keep doing this. I'm drowning in it.

My business isn't growing. I'm not getting ahead. Hell, I'm not even getting any sleep!"

Now, I've seen this a million times, so I wasn't surprised. I could tell right away that Mike was caught in the trap of *doing* everything. But here's the kicker—Mike didn't even realize what he was doing. He thought he was just doing what needed to be done to keep the lights on. What he didn't realize was that he was trying to be the entrepreneur, the manager, and the technician all at once—and that's a recipe for disaster.

So, I sat Mike down and started to break it down for him. I said, "Mike, let's get one thing straight. You can't be the *guy* that fixes everything, runs the day-to-day, *and* sets the vision for your business all at the same time. That's like trying to play all the positions on a football team. You can't be quarterback, running back, and the guy holding the chains at the same time."

He looked at me like I had two heads. He said, "But I *have* to do it all. I'm the only one who can fix these technical problems. I'm the one talking to the clients. I don't have the money to hire anyone!"

That's when it clicked. He was doing it all, and no surprise—he wasn't getting anywhere. He was juggling the technician role—fixing technical issues. The manager role—dealing with day-to-day operations and finances. And the entrepreneur role—driving the business forward with the vision and strategy. The result? Nothing was getting done to its full potential.

So, I broke it down further. "Look, Mike, as a technician, you're great at solving problems. But you're also the manager, and your team (you) needs guidance, structure, and leadership. You're the one making sure the gears are turning, and things are running smoothly. And as the entrepreneur, your job is to step back, set the long-term vision, and think strategically about where the business should go. You've got to wear all three hats, but not at the same time. That's the problem. You're trying to run the company while building it. The CEO can't just be the worker bee."

It was like a lightbulb went off. He started to get it. The entrepreneur role was about looking at the business from a bird's-eye view—*strategizing, planning, and setting direction*. The manager role was about *making sure the systems were in place*, the team was supported, and things ran smoothly day-to-day. And the technician role—well, that's the workhorse. The person who's doing the actual, hands-on work. It's fine to do technician work, but not *all the time*. If Mike kept trying to be the technician every day, his business would stagnate.

So, we got to work. We started breaking down his tasks, separating the roles, and making a plan to start delegating more. We carved out time for him to think like the entrepreneur and set clear goals for the business. We made sure he wasn't buried in the trenches, managing everything by the seat of his pants. And slowly, but surely, Mike started to gain control of his business again.

The key takeaway here is simple: If you're running your business and you're doing all the work, you're never going to move forward. You have to separate the roles and give yourself permission to be the entrepreneur. That means focusing on the bigger picture, delegating the day-to-day, and stepping out of the technician's shoes. Once Mike understood that, things started clicking. He started leading, not just doing.

Here's the deal: *Every successful business has three distinct roles— entrepreneur, manager, and technician.* If you try to do all three at once, you'll burn out. Period. You need to recognize which role you're playing at any given moment, and then be strategic about it.

So, here's your action step: Take a hard look at your day. Are you wearing too many hats? Are you spreading yourself too thin? Stop being the technician and start being the entrepreneur. It's time to take a step back, get out of the weeds, and start running your business, not just working in it.

The Entrepreneur

Let's break down the entrepreneur role for a second. First off, Michael Gerber introduced this concept in *The E-Myth Revisited,* and trust me, it's one of the most important ideas in business that people tend to overlook. The entrepreneur role is the big-picture thinker. It's the person who doesn't just get their hands dirty with the day-to-day grind. Instead, they're focused on the *why* of the business, the strategy, and the vision. They're the ones looking into the future, figuring out where the business should go and how it should grow.

Now, let's be real here—this isn't the fun part of business. It's not about getting high-fives from customers or solving immediate problems. It's about planning for the long-term. It's about stepping back from the daily chaos and thinking: *What's the next step? What do I want my business to look like in 5 years?* The entrepreneur's job is to set the direction, build the framework, and keep the business aligned with the bigger vision.

Think of it like being the driver of a car. The entrepreneur is the one who's sitting behind the wheel, looking ahead and saying, "Alright, we're heading down this road, and here's where I want to go." They're not worried about the fact that the car needs gas or that the tires are losing air. They're not knee-deep in the weeds of fixing the engine or cleaning the car. Those are other roles. The entrepreneur's job is to steer the damn thing toward the destination. If you want your business to go somewhere meaningful, the entrepreneur is the one who has to make sure you're heading in the right direction.

Now, I know, you're probably thinking, *"That sounds nice, Eric, but I can't afford to stop working in my business. The bills are due, and there's no one else to do the work."* Here's the problem: You'll never get your business to scale or function without the entrepreneur mindset. If you're constantly in the trenches, solving every single issue, putting out every fire, and drowning in the day-to-day grind, you're never going to get out of that hamster wheel. You'll be stuck, and your business will reflect that.

Gerber talks about working *on* the business, not *in* it. When you take a step back and start acting as the entrepreneur, you're thinking long-term, setting systems in place, and aligning everything to make sure your business can thrive without you having to micromanage it. That's the magic of the entrepreneur role. It's about putting processes in place that keep things running smoothly without needing to be involved in every little detail. It's about building a business that works without you being there all the time.

For instance, look at how successful franchises operate. Think about McDonald's. You don't need the founder flipping burgers to make it work. There's a system. There's a blueprint. And that blueprint is designed by someone in the entrepreneur role. The business runs on systems, and those systems don't require a hands-on entrepreneur to run. When you stop acting like a technician and start thinking like the entrepreneur, you can begin to build those same systems for your business, allowing it to scale.

The entrepreneur role is about vision. It's about leadership. It's about creating a roadmap for your business and setting it up for long-term success. This isn't about you working harder—it's about you working smarter and laying down the groundwork for others to take the reins when needed. When you nail this role, you'll stop putting out fires and start building something sustainable. But to do that, you need to think like the entrepreneur, act like the entrepreneur, and put in the work to create a business that runs on systems, not sweat.

So, if you're reading this and you're still stuck in the weeds of the day-to-day, trying to do everything at once, it's time to step into the entrepreneur role. You're going to have to let go of some control, and yes, it's going to feel uncomfortable at first, but once you get it, the business will start to run itself—and that's when the magic happens.

The Manager

Alright, now that we've nailed down the entrepreneur role, let's talk about the manager. This is the person who's in charge of making sure things run smoothly on the day-to-day. Think of the manager as the one who takes the entrepreneur's vision and actually puts it into action. They're the ones responsible for making sure everything is organized, the systems are running, and things are moving forward without the chaos. If the entrepreneur is the one steering the ship, the manager is the one making sure there's fuel in the tank, the sails are up, and the crew knows exactly what they're doing.

But here's the thing: the manager isn't always the most glamorous role in the business. It's not about having the big ideas, creating the vision, or setting long-term goals. The manager's role is more about the implementation of those ideas. They're focused on processes, people, and productivity. They're making sure that everything works as it should, that there's clear communication, and that everyone is doing their part.

When you're in this role, you're focused on the systems the entrepreneur has set up and making sure they function like well-oiled machinery. You're the one solving problems in real-time, keeping things running, and making sure the business is working as it should in the present. You're essentially the glue that holds everything together. The entrepreneur might be looking five steps ahead, but the manager is making sure the next step is being taken right now.

This is where a lot of business owners get stuck. They're caught between being the entrepreneur and the manager, trying to drive the vision forward while also making sure the day-to-day operations aren't falling apart. And trust me, I've been there. I've worn both hats, and I can tell you, it's exhausting. When you're juggling both roles, it's easy to burn out. You're working on big-picture ideas and handling the grind all at once—and that's when things start to slip through the cracks.

But when you understand that you need to step into the manager role at certain times, it all starts to make sense. You start to recognize that your job as a manager isn't just about making sure everyone's busy; it's about making sure they're busy with purpose. It's about setting clear expectations, putting systems in place, and following up to make sure things are actually happening. If you want your business to run smoothly and consistently, you need a strong manager role that keeps the wheels turning while the entrepreneur's looking forward.

So, what does this mean for you? If you want your business to scale and grow, it's time to let the entrepreneur dream while you take care of the details. Set up systems, manage your team effectively, and make sure everything is aligned with the big-picture goals. If you can nail this balance, your business will run like a well-oiled machine—and you'll be able to step away from the daily grind to focus on the bigger stuff.

The Technician

Now we've talked about the entrepreneur and the manager. But there's one more critical piece of the puzzle—the technician. This is the role that most people get stuck in, especially when you're starting out in business. The technician is the doer. The one who's hands-on, getting stuff done, and turning all the ideas into reality. When you first start a business, you probably find yourself slipping into this role without even thinking about it. It's natural—you have to wear many hats in the beginning. But the technician's role is where the rubber meets the road, and honestly, it's where most people get bogged down.

Think about it: when you first start your business, it's easy to get caught up in the day-to-day tasks. You're the one doing the work, whether that's designing the product, handling customer service, or managing the production. You're running the show, but you're stuck in the weeds. It's exhausting, and it doesn't leave much room for strategic thinking or growth. And that's where things start to break down.

When you get caught in the technician role, you're stuck doing the work instead of running the business. You're working *in* the business, not *on* the business. You're knee-deep in the tasks, but you're not thinking about the bigger picture. You're not setting the vision or managing the systems. You're just grinding it out. And while grinding is important, it's not sustainable in the long run. At some point, you need to step back, delegate, and free yourself from the day-to-day grind so you can focus on the bigger picture.

Here's the kicker: if you stay in the technician role for too long, you're going to burn out. You're going to reach a point where you're overwhelmed, overworked, and you start resenting the very thing you built. It's the classic "I wanted to be my own boss, but now I feel like I'm working for my business" scenario. The technician's role is crucial, but it's not meant to be a permanent fixture. It's a role you need to learn to step out of if you want to grow your business.

So, what do you do about it? First, you need to get clear on what the technician role is in your business. What tasks are you spending your time on? Are they things that only you can do, or are there others on your team who can handle some of that load? Once you identify the tasks, start delegating. The entrepreneur in you needs to dream big, the manager needs to put systems in place, and the technician needs to take a step back and let others handle the day-to-day operations.

If you're going to scale your business, you can't do everything yourself. You can't wear all three hats forever. You need to build a team, develop systems, and focus on being the visionary leader your business needs. If you can step out of the technician role, your business will be free to grow, and you'll be able to shift your focus where it matters most—on leading the charge, creating value, and ensuring the long-term success of your company.

Final Thoughts

Understanding the entrepreneur, manager, and technician roles isn't just about theory—it's the foundation of building a business that actually works. Each role is critical, but trying to wear all three hats simultaneously will leave you exhausted, overwhelmed, and spinning your wheels.

Now's the time to reflect: Which role are you stuck in? Are you buried in technician tasks, grinding away without room to think strategically? Are you juggling the details as a manager but struggling to lift your head and dream big as an entrepreneur? Wherever you're stuck, recognize it—and take action to rebalance.

The secret to a thriving business isn't being the hero who does it all. It's understanding where you're needed most and empowering others to fill in the gaps. When you can step into the entrepreneur's shoes to dream and strategize, rely on the manager to implement systems, and let the technicians execute, your business will start to move like a well-oiled machine.

So, take a moment to think about where you're spending your time. Are you leading your business, managing it effectively, or getting stuck in the grind? The next chapter will help you put this knowledge into action, but for now, remember: The magic happens when all three roles align, and you focus on what only *you* can do to move your business forward. Let's keep building.

Let's Put This Into Action

"Help me define and separate the three main roles in my business: the Entrepreneur, the Manager, and the Technician. I need clear guidance on how to identify the responsibilities for each role and how to balance them effectively. Break down what tasks fall under each role, and give me actionable steps for how to move from wearing all the hats to delegating and focusing on the right role at the right time. Help me understand where I need to focus more as the Entrepreneur, and how I can build systems to handle the Manager and Technician duties."

This prompt will help you clarify your role as a business owner, delegate tasks appropriately, and create a more balanced and efficient structure for your business. It will guide you toward the proper mindset and actions to grow your company without getting bogged down in every single responsibility.

☆★☆

Chapter 6:

SYSTEMS

Let me tell you something: The U.S. Army is the greatest fighting force in the world, and I'm not just saying that because I've spent most of my life in it—though I've got plenty of reasons to back it up. One of the big reasons we kick so much ass is because we've got systems in place. Systems, my friend, are what separate the pros from the amateurs, and the Army gets it right with something every successful business needs: Standard Operating Procedures (SOPs).

I've worked with military units from several other countries, and let me tell you—they're a disaster when it comes to organizing themselves. Every single unit had its own way of doing things. No consistency. No standard procedures. It's like trying to play a team sport where every player has their own playbook, and some of them don't even know the rules.

I'll give you an example. I once worked with a partner nation's military that didn't have SOPs for anything. Soldiers showed up in different uniforms, stood in formation differently, and when they were training, they all had different ways to react to contact. Now, here's the thing: combat amplifies that chaos. When multiple units are involved in an operation and none of them follow the same procedures, people start to make mistakes. And that's how lives get lost. You need consistency to make sure everyone's on the same page and that they've got each other's back. Without it, you're just asking for disaster.

Then you roll into a U.S. Army unit, and it's a whole different story. We've got SOPs for everything—convoy procedures, packing lists, gear checks, maintenance—hell, one unit I was in even had an SOP for how to tie your boots. These SOPs aren't just about making sure everyone's on the same page—they're about making sure when a unit gets swapped out or a soldier gets assigned to a new post, they can plug right in and hit the ground running without a hitch. They don't need to reinvent the wheel. They follow a system that's been proven to work.

So, here's where it gets interesting. When I first became a platoon sergeant, I joined a new unit. I'll never forget my first day. The commander looks me dead in the eye and says, "We've never had a convoy leave on time." I asked, "Why?" He said they didn't have SOPs. I stared at him for a second and thought, "Alright, time to fix this." We couldn't be operating like amateurs anymore. No more rolling the dice and hoping things work out.

So, I went to work. I started creating SOPs. I didn't care if it was something simple like the order of the trucks, who was in each one, or what equipment went where. I made sure every little detail was covered: the radios for each truck, the exact driving speeds, which vehicle would be the recovery truck if something went wrong. I worked with the convoy commander to map everything out—precision was key. We needed to know exactly what was going on at all times.

And guess what? The very next convoy we ran, we were ready to roll an hour early. No joke. Because we knew exactly what to expect from every truck, every driver, and every security team member. Everything was planned, standardized, and most importantly, everyone was on the same page. No scrambling at the last minute, no wondering who was doing what, and certainly no one forgetting their gear. It was smooth. And when you're on a convoy, smooth means safe.

Now, why am I telling you this? Because that's exactly how systems work in business. You don't need to reinvent the wheel every time a problem pops up. You need systems—processes that can be followed again and again, no matter what. The Army thrives because they can move troops and gear around with minimal friction. They follow SOPs that tell them exactly what to do, organizational SOPs like Army Regulations (ARs) and Field Manuals (FM) or unit SOPs like Tactical SOPs (TACSOPs). It's the same with your business. You need systems that allow your team to work efficiently and effectively, whether they've been there for years or just started last week.

I know what some of you are thinking: "But I don't want my business to be all rigid and rule-bound! I want some flexibility!" Sure, you need flexibility. But that doesn't mean throwing out the playbook. Flexibility is great, but only when you have a solid foundation. SOPs give you that foundation. They give your business the structure it needs to scale, so you're not constantly putting out fires.

Here's the takeaway: your business needs systems. You can't just wing it and expect everything to run smoothly. Whether it's managing your team, fulfilling orders, handling customer service, or even marketing—everything should be standardized. When you have SOPs in place, everyone knows what to do. It's like a well-oiled machine that keeps running even when you're not looking over everyone's shoulder. Trust me, the alternative is pure chaos.

So, take a good look at your business. What systems can you put in place today to get everyone on the same page and moving in the right direction? The more streamlined your processes are, the more your business will run like a professional outfit, not a three-ring circus. And when you've got that kind of clarity, you'll be able to scale, pivot, and grow your business without losing your mind.

So, what makes a good system?

Alright, now that we've established just how disastrous it can be when you're running a business without systems, let's get to the good stuff—what actually makes a good system?

Because here's the thing: systems aren't some magical "set it and forget it" kind of thing. If you're thinking you can just slap a few processes together, cross your fingers, and hope it all works out, you're about to be sorely disappointed. No, no, no. A good system is like your most reliable soldier. It's the one who shows up on time, does what it's supposed to, and doesn't need a million reminders. It's there to back you up when the going gets tough and keeps things running smoothly when you're ready to take a step back and breathe.

But what makes a system *good*? Well, it's not about complexity or having a million moving parts. A good system is simple, repeatable, and scalable. It's designed to get the job done efficiently and with as little drama as possible. When you put a system in place, it should make things run smoother, save you time, and keep you from micromanaging every little detail. Think of it like having a solid battle plan. It's not about making everything perfect, it's about having the right structure so you can handle whatever comes your way without panicking.

A good system, whether it's for inventory, staff roles, or customer service, is predictable. You know what to expect, and so does everyone else involved. When your system works, you can focus on growing the business instead of always getting bogged down by the daily grind. And, most importantly, systems give you room to step out of the weeds and work on your business rather than just being stuck in it.

Alright, let's break down what a good system really looks like. If you want to run a business that doesn't feel like a three-ring circus, you need systems that check the right boxes. Here's what you're looking for:

1. Simplicity.

First and foremost, a good system doesn't need to be complicated. Too often, business owners overcomplicate things thinking that more moving parts equals more efficiency. That's not the case. A simple system is easy to train your team on, easy to tweak when things go wrong, and—most importantly—easy to scale. If your system requires a PhD to understand, it's not a system; it's a nightmare in the making. Think of it like a fire drill: it's simple, straightforward, and everyone knows what to do when the bell rings.

2. Consistency.

A good system ensures that things get done the same way, every time. Consistency is key. If your team doesn't know how to do something, or if different people are doing the same task in totally different ways, you're setting yourself up for failure. A solid system ensures everyone follows the same process, which makes it easier to track progress and pinpoint problems. This is how you avoid the "well, we did it this way last time, why didn't it work this time?" scenario. Consistency also helps build trust with your customers. They'll know exactly what to expect, and that reliability will keep them coming back.

3. Accountability.

Who's responsible for what? If your system doesn't have clear roles and responsibilities, it's like sending a bunch of people on a treasure hunt without a map. Everyone's scrambling, no one knows who's doing what, and in the end, you're lucky if you find the treasure at all. Good systems clearly define who's responsible for what at every stage of the process. If someone drops the ball, you can trace it back to the specific part of the system, figure out why it failed, and fix it. It's like a well-organized military operation—everyone knows their role and executes their part of the plan with precision.

4. Flexibility (But Not Too Much).

Now, hold up—this doesn't mean you throw out the rulebook and start winging it. But you also need to be flexible enough to make adjustments when things change. The world of business moves fast, and what worked last week might not be the best solution this week.

So, a good system should allow for small adjustments without breaking down entirely. Just like the military uses the "adapt and overcome" mentality, your business system should be able to evolve with the times. But here's the key: don't confuse flexibility with chaos. Flexibility means adjusting the system as needed, not reinventing the whole damn thing every time you hit a roadblock.

5. Automation.

Lastly, a good system has the ability to automate as much as possible. The less human error you have, the better. If your system relies on people remembering to do things every time, you're going to have problems. Good systems will automate repetitive tasks, like invoicing, scheduling, and follow-ups, leaving your team to focus on more critical tasks. It's like having a robot assistant that handles the boring stuff, so your people can focus on the big picture. The less you have to worry about the little things, the more time you have to grow the business.

When you've got a system in place that has all these elements—simplicity, consistency, accountability, flexibility, and automation—you're setting yourself up for success. Your business will run smoother, your team will be more efficient, and you won't spend your days putting out fires or chasing your tail. This is the foundation that allows you to scale, improve, and get your business working for you, not the other way around.

How to Create Systems?

Alright, now that we know what makes a good system—SOPs, simplicity, consistency, accountability, flexibility, and automation—

let's talk about how to actually create it. It's time to roll up your sleeves, stop daydreaming about that beach vacation, and get to work.

Creating a system isn't some mystical process that only the lucky few get to master. It's a step-by-step grind that, once you get it right, will save you more time, energy, and headaches than you can imagine. Trust me—your future self will thank you for putting in the work now. So, how do you get started? Grab a pen, a whiteboard, or whatever tool works for you, and let's start laying out the blueprint. Here's the process.

1. **Identify the Core Functions**: Start by pinpointing the main areas of your business that need systems. Think of the tasks that keep popping up regularly—things like managing customer orders, processing payments, handling customer service inquiries, or even onboarding new employees. These are the core functions you need to build systems for. If you're running a restaurant, for example, you'll want to start with systems for food prep, order taking, and customer service. Don't try to do everything at once—just focus on the big, recurring tasks first.

2. **Create Standard Operating Procedures (SOPs)**: SOPs are the foundation of any strong system. They're the rules of engagement—the "how-to" guide for your business. Write down clear, simple steps for completing tasks in each core function. Make it as detailed as necessary, but don't make it so complex that nobody will actually follow it. The goal here is clarity. For example, if you're writing an SOP for taking customer orders, don't leave anything to chance. Specify how the order should be taken, what information needs to be confirmed with the customer, and how it should be processed in the

system. SOPs should remove ambiguity and give your team clear guidelines on how to get things done.

Case Study:

Studies show businesses with SOPs see 25% higher productivity—proof your squad can scale without burning out. A landscaping company with a 6-person team struggled as new clients overwhelmed their process. The owner handled every inquiry, leading to missed follow-ups and frustrated customers. After implementing an onboarding SOP, they assigned a point person to log 10 inquiries weekly into their CRM, cutting response time from 72 to 24 hours. The team's needs assessment calls uncovered 80% of clients wanted faster deliverables, prompting a streamlined proposal process. Within three months, client satisfaction rose from 70% to 90%, and the owner reclaimed 10 hours weekly to focus on strategy. The use of SOPs transformed their squad into a client-ready machine.

3. **Simplify**: You don't need 10-page documents to explain how to take an order. Get to the point. People are busy, so your systems should be easy to follow and efficient. Don't get bogged down in overcomplicating things. The simpler your systems are, the more likely they are to be followed. If your team is drowning in instructions, they're going to shut down. Keep it simple, stupid—this is about making things easier, not harder.

4. **Automate Where Possible**: Here's where the magic happens. Once you've got your core systems in place, look for places where you can automate tasks. Whether it's through software, apps, or tools, automation can take a huge load off your shoulders. For example, you can automate customer follow-ups through an email system, or use a

POS system that sends orders directly to the kitchen, cutting out the middleman. Automation makes your systems run smoother, and the less you're involved in the day-to-day tasks, the more time you have to focus on growing the business.

5. **Test & Refine**: Don't expect everything to be perfect on the first try. Your systems will likely need tweaking as you go along. That's fine. The goal here is to get something in place that works, then refine it over time. Test your systems, gather feedback from your team, and make adjustments where necessary. Systems aren't static—they're living, breathing things that evolve as your business grows. Don't be afraid to change things up when you see areas for improvement.

6. **Delegate & Hold People Accountable**: This is the part where most business owners fall flat. They create systems, but then they try to do everything themselves. That's not the point. Your systems are meant to take tasks off your plate, not add more. Once your systems are in place, delegate the tasks to your team and hold them accountable for following the SOPs. If someone isn't doing their part, address it— don't just let it slide. Your business runs on consistency, so everyone needs to pull their weight.

7. **Review & Optimize**: After your systems are running, keep checking in. Are there new opportunities for automation? Can tasks be streamlined further? What's working well, and what isn't? The best systems evolve over time, so always be on the lookout for ways to make them even more efficient.

Alright, here's the final piece of the puzzle: when you're first starting out with building systems, it's all about focusing on the low-hanging fruit. Start with the technician tasks—those are the things that eat up your time the most. These are the tasks that you can easily delegate once they're standardized. For example, if you're running a restaurant, start with something simple like the process for taking orders or prepping food. These tasks don't require deep managerial thinking; they just need to be done consistently. So, create clear SOPs for these technician tasks and start delegating them. The goal here is to free up your time so you can step into the manager role—where you can start overseeing things, making sure everything's running smoothly, and tweaking your systems as needed.

Once the technician tasks are under control, move on to creating SOPs for your manager role. These are the tasks that require oversight—things like managing your team, keeping track of inventory, and handling customer service complaints. With SOPs in place for your managerial tasks, you'll start spending more time on high-level strategy and growth.

And finally, as your business becomes more organized and efficient, you'll find yourself spending most of your time in the entrepreneur role—the visionary, the strategist, the big-picture thinker. This is where you want to be. When you've built a solid system, you're no longer stuck in the weeds. You can focus on growing your business, developing new opportunities, and creating the future you envision.

So, in short: start with the low-hanging fruit. Create systems for those technician tasks. Delegate them. Move on to the manager tasks. Delegate those, too. And then, with your time freed up, focus on the entrepreneur role—the role where the real growth happens. That's how you build a business that works for you, not the other way around.

Common Pitfalls to Avoid

Alright, now that we've got a good sense of how to start building your systems, let's talk about the landmines you'll want to avoid. It's easy to get excited about systems, thinking you're about to create the perfect, shiny, well-oiled machine. But trust me, the road to success is littered with pitfalls. You've got to know what they are so you don't end up knee-deep in chaos all over again, wondering where you went wrong.

The truth is, even with the best intentions, it's not always smooth sailing. You'll hit snags—systems that sound good in theory but don't quite work in practice, tasks that look simple but are harder than they seem, or just the overwhelming task of trying to create a system for every single thing in your business. So, let's go through a few of the classic mistakes I see all the time. Get ready to dodge them like a pro.

1. Overcomplicating Things from the Start

Listen, I get it—you're excited, you want to make everything perfect, so you try to create a system for every single thing in your business. You're diving into fancy software, overthinking the processes, and trying to design something that's going to solve every problem at once. But guess what? You've just built a maze for yourself and your team to get lost in.

The fix? Keep it simple. Start with the basics and get a solid system in place before adding layers. Think of it like building a house—lay down the foundation first, and don't go installing the chandelier before you've got the walls up. Start small, focus on what actually needs to be done right now, and expand from there as you get comfortable.

2. Ignoring the People Who Will Use the System

Systems don't exist in a vacuum. The tech, the tools, the processes—they're only as good as the people using them. If you're creating a system but not involving the people who actually have to use it on the ground, then you're wasting everyone's time. They'll ignore it, resent it, or worse, do things the old way anyway.

The fix? Involve your team from the start. Get their input. Ask what works, what doesn't, and what could make their lives easier. Get buy-in. After all, it's their daily grind, not yours. A system is only effective if it's practical and actually adopted by the people who need to use it.

3. Trying to Create Systems for Everything All at Once

Like I said before, it's tempting to just go full throttle and create systems for every little thing. You'll end up spending so much time on this, and guess what happens? You'll neglect your actual business. The daily operations won't be running smoothly because you're buried in documentation, processes, and tech tools that still aren't quite right.

The fix? Start with the low-hanging fruit—those easy wins that don't take much time or effort but have a big impact. Focus on areas where systems will free up the most time or eliminate the biggest bottlenecks. Maybe it's the order process, or maybe it's tracking employee hours. Whatever it is, prioritize systems that immediately reduce chaos. Once you've got those in place, you'll have more time and energy to focus on bigger, more complex systems.

4. Neglecting to Test and Refine the System

If you set up a system and just leave it without checking in on it, you're asking for trouble. The first version of your system won't be perfect. It'll need tweaking. It'll need to evolve as your business grows. If you think you can set it and forget it, you're in for a rude awakening.

The fix? Test, evaluate, and refine. Don't just assume everything will be fine once it's in place. Check in with the people using the system regularly. Track performance. Tweak the processes as needed. Think of it like a workout plan—you don't just hit the gym once and call it a day. You adjust, refine, and improve based on what's working (and what's not).

5. Failing to Align the System with Your Bigger Goals

A system is only effective if it helps you achieve the bigger goals of your business. You can't just set up a bunch of processes for the sake of having processes. They need to align with where you want to go. Otherwise, you're just spinning your wheels and wasting time.

The fix? Always tie your systems back to your larger business goals. If you're focusing on scaling, make sure your systems are built to support that. If you're trying to improve customer satisfaction, align your customer service processes to ensure that happens. Every system should have a purpose that's in line with what you're working to achieve.

6. Letting Perfection Stop Progress

Look, I get it. Nobody likes to roll something out that's imperfect, but guess what? Waiting for the system to be "perfect" before implementing it means you'll never get anything done. You'll be stuck in an endless loop of tweaking and never actually solving the problem. Your systems don't need to be flawless—they just need to work.

The fix? Start with a solid version of the system and launch it. Don't aim for perfection. Aim for progress. You can always improve and tweak it later. Perfecting a system over time is better than never having it in place at all. Don't be that person who spends six months planning and never executes. That's a recipe for disaster.

Final Thoughts

That's a wrap on the systems chapter. Here's the thing: running a business without systems is like trying to fight a war with no plan. Chaos, confusion, and a whole lot of wasted effort. But when you have a solid system in place, you're not just fighting fires—you're strategizing, executing, and winning.

Systems are the backbone of your business. They give you clarity when the chaos sets in. They keep your operations running smoothly, your team aligned, and your business scaling without constantly needing you to be in the trenches. The truth is, if you don't put these systems in place, you're just running around putting out fires and wondering why nothing gets done.

Start small, stay consistent, and keep tweaking as you go. Don't try to perfect everything right out the gate. Just get things rolling, and before you know it, your systems will start working for you instead of you working for them.

If you want to go from surviving to thriving, you've got to get your systems locked down. Once that's in place, you'll be able to focus on growing your business, hitting your goals, and stepping back from the daily grind so you can focus on the bigger picture.

Now go ahead and start building those systems. You'll thank yourself later when things aren't such a mess, and you're not stuck in the weeds every single day. Trust me—once you get a taste of running a business that's actually organized, you'll wonder how you ever did it without them. Keep it simple, keep it smart, and most importantly, keep moving forward. Let's go get this business in gear.

Let's Put This Into Action

A.I. takes your Operations to the next level by automating repetitive tasks and optimizing workflows. Tools like Zapier or Make can connect your apps—say, syncing customer orders from your website to your inventory system without manual entry. For a restaurant owner, A.I. scheduling software can predict busy hours based on past data and staff your shifts accordingly, cutting labor costs while keeping service smooth. The A.I. prompt below will guide you to identify tasks ripe for automation, freeing you to focus on strategy over grunt work.

"Help me create systems for my business and determine what tools can automate [tasks] for my business. I need a clear plan to build and implement processes that will streamline operations, improve efficiency, and reduce chaos. Start by focusing on the areas where I can delegate and automate tasks, such as customer onboarding, inventory

management and order fulfillment. Break down each process into actionable steps, assign responsibilities, and make sure there's a clear way to track and measure success. Help me prioritize these systems so I can spend more time focusing on the bigger picture, while ensuring everything runs smoothly day-to-day."

This prompt will help you get your business organized, establish smooth workflows, and save you time—so you can focus on building the business you really want without constantly drowning in the day-to-day chaos.

Bonus

I know we've covered a lot in this chapter, and the idea of creating systems might feel like a big task to tackle. But here's the reality: 70% of small businesses lack standardized processes, leading to inefficiencies that choke growth. That's why I've got you covered. To make it easier, I've created a simple SOP template—the exact framework I use with my clients to get their businesses running like clockwork.

This template will save you time, headaches, and guesswork. All you need to do is fill in the blanks and customize it for your business. Head over to my website https://tgscoaching.com/resources/ and grab your copy today. Don't want to type? No problem—just scan the QR code below and get started.

This is your first step toward building systems that work for you, not the other way around. I know you're going to find it super useful!

☆★☆

Chapter 7:

FINANCIAL MANAGEMENT

Let me take you back to one of the rougher patches of my business coaching career. I had this client, let's call him Bob. Bob owned a small construction company, and like most business owners, he had big dreams. He had the whole thing mapped out in his head—expand his team, scale up, maybe even move into bigger markets. But there was one little problem: Bob didn't have a clue when it came to financial management.

He had the enthusiasm of a guy who just chugged three Red Bulls, but when it came to cash flow, budgeting, and financial strategy, it was like watching a dog try to solve a Rubik's cube—completely clueless.

Bob would call me every week in a panic, asking where the money was going. He had more "leads" than he knew what to do with, so business was good on paper. But every time I asked him about cash flow or expenses, he gave me the same look that a deer gives when it's caught in headlights. No budgeting, no financial plan. It was a lot of work, but nothing ever seemed to stick.

One day, after a couple of months of seeing the same problems pop up over and over, Bob called me in a frenzy. "I can't make payroll, man. What the hell is going on?" he asked, nearly hyperventilating. I went over to his office, and he handed me a stack of invoices, receipts, and bank statements—nothing organized, just piles of paper. It looked like a tornado had swept through his accounting department.

After about an hour of trying to make sense of the chaos, I asked, "Bob, where's your budget?"

He looked at me like I'd just asked him to solve a crossword puzzle in Russian. "Budget?" he replied, like I was speaking another language. "Isn't that what accountants do?"

I had to pause and collect myself. "No, Bob. Budgeting is what keeps you from running your business like a wild animal. You need to know where your money is going, how much you're spending, and how much you can expect to make, or you'll end up in the same position you're in now—unable to pay people, scrambling for cash, and getting calls from your suppliers asking where their money is."

He stared at me blankly for a second. I could see the wheels turning in his head. "Okay, so what do I do?"

Here's where the hard truth comes in. "Bob, you need to understand cash flow. It's like blood in your business' veins. Without it, your company's dead in the water. You can't just keep spending money like you're Rockefeller. You have to plan your expenses, set aside funds for emergencies, and make sure you're not outpacing your revenue."

We spent the next few hours working through some of his financial systems. I walked him through setting up a basic cash flow spreadsheet that tracked his incoming and outgoing funds, and we built a simple budget to make sure he wasn't throwing money around willy-nilly. It wasn't rocket science. We broke down his recurring costs—his payroll, equipment, supplies, and materials—and then forecasted his incoming revenue based on the leads he was actually closing. I made him understand that budgeting isn't about constraining growth, but about creating a framework that allows your business to expand sustainably.

Then we talked about strategy. Financial strategy, to be specific. A strategy isn't just having a plan; it's about making intentional, informed decisions. Bob didn't need to keep taking on every project that came his way. We focused on the ones that were most profitable, rather than just trying to chase after everything. We worked on cutting out unnecessary overheads and focusing on improving the core parts of his business. I told him that a good financial strategy isn't about being cheap; it's about being smart. Spending where it counts and trimming the fat where possible.

A few weeks later, Bob called me up again—this time, not in a panic. "You won't believe this," he said, "but we actually have money in the bank this month. I'm paying my guys on time, and we're actually making a profit."

That, my friend, is the power of understanding your finances. Cash flow isn't some abstract concept; it's the lifeblood of your business. Budgeting isn't just something you do because your accountant says so; it's how you keep your business from crashing and burning. And a financial strategy? That's your roadmap. Without it, you're just driving around aimlessly, hoping you don't hit a dead end.

The key takeaway here is simple: without a solid grasp on cash flow, budgeting, and a strategic financial plan, you're setting yourself up for failure. If Bob can get his financial house in order, so can you. The rest of this book is going to help you get to a point where money isn't something that keeps you up at night. Instead, you'll be using it to fuel your growth and your future.

And trust me, you don't want to learn this lesson the hard way like Bob did—no one's got the time for that.

So, what is good financial management?

Alright, now that we've seen the mess Bob got himself into by not paying attention to his financial systems, let's talk about how to actually get a handle on things before you end up in the same boat.

Good financial management isn't just about tracking receipts and praying that the money magically shows up in your bank account. It's about having a clear understanding of where your money's going, how much you're making, and what you need to keep your business alive and growing. You've got to build a financial strategy that works for you, not just throw some numbers together and hope for the best. Trust me, if you do that, you'll end up in a worse spot than Bob was.

So, what does good financial management look like? It's more than just knowing your cash flow, although that's a big part of it. It's about creating systems for budgeting, forecasting, and setting up controls to ensure you don't end up living paycheck to paycheck as a business owner. If you've ever had that "uh-oh" moment where you realize you spent more than you made and now you're scrambling, then you know exactly what I'm talking about. A solid financial strategy puts you in control instead of the other way around.

Alright, let's break this down into the key pieces of good financial management. These are the things you need to keep track of and make sure they're solid so you don't end up in Bob's situation.

1. Cash Flow Management:

This is the lifeblood of your business. Cash flow is the money coming in and going out—what you earn versus what you spend. If you're not paying attention to it, you could be making money on paper, but still be broke because there's no cash in the bank when you need it. You've got to know what's coming in, what's going out, and when. If you can get your hands on software to automate some of this, do it. But even if you're using a spreadsheet, make sure you have a pulse on your cash flow. Monitor it weekly, monthly, and quarterly. If you're spending more than you're bringing in, then you better have a plan on how to close that gap.

2. Budgeting:

This is where you start to get proactive instead of reactive. A budget is essentially your game plan for how you're going to allocate the money you have and make sure you're not overspending. You've got to set clear limits on things like operating costs, salaries, marketing expenses, and any other overhead. Don't just guess—sit down, plan, and stick to it. That budget is your road map, and without it, you're driving blind. Keep it flexible, but be sure you're checking against it regularly. If you start veering off course, that's a sign you need to adjust your approach.

3. Financial Forecasting:

You wouldn't go on a road trip without a map, right? Forecasting is your map for the future of your business. You need to predict your revenue, your costs, and cash flow over the next year, at least. And I'm not just talking about crossing your fingers and hoping you make more money. This is about understanding where your business is going and having a solid strategy in place for how you'll grow, how you'll handle expenses, and how you'll respond to any changes in the market or economy. If you can, get someone who knows how to forecast, but if you're doing it on your own, get familiar with tools or templates that can help. It's about being prepared and thinking ahead, so you're not blindsided when things change.

4. Profit Margins & Pricing Strategy:

You want to know what you're making off each sale, right? If you're running a business that's selling a product or service, your profit margin is critical. You need to understand how much it costs to produce whatever you're selling and how much profit you're making on each item. Without this, you're running blind and likely not charging enough—or worse, overcharging your customers and losing sales. Make sure you're setting your prices strategically, so you can hit your goals while also keeping customers happy.

5. Emergency Fund & Debt Management:

Life happens, businesses hit speed bumps. You need an emergency fund that will cover unexpected costs or dips in cash flow. This might be harder in the beginning, but once your business starts stabilizing, it's crucial to have reserves to draw from. As for debt—don't let it spiral out of control. If you're borrowing to fund your business, understand exactly how much you owe, the terms of repayment, and how the debt affects your cash flow. Pay attention to the interest, and always look for ways to reduce that burden over time.

6. Financial Reporting and Metrics:

Look, you can't improve what you don't measure. If you're not regularly reviewing your income statement, balance sheet, and cash flow statements, you're just guessing. These reports will give you the cold, hard facts about where your business stands. Start reviewing them monthly, and get familiar with key metrics—like your gross margin, operating expenses, and net profit. If numbers aren't your thing, then find someone who can break them down for you, but you've got to understand the financial health of your business.

So, now that we've laid it all out, you're probably wondering, "Where do I start?" The truth is, don't wait until you're knee-deep in the chaos. Start with a strong foundation. Track your cash flow, budget your expenses, and get a handle on your pricing strategy. As you grow, add in forecasting and emergency funds. This isn't just about being financially savvy, it's about keeping your business running smoothly and positioning yourself for growth instead of a financial disaster.

How to create it?

Now that we've got the basics of financial management down, let's talk about how to take all this and create a solid financial strategy that'll keep your business on track and growing.

Creating a financial strategy is like building a roadmap for your business. You wouldn't drive across the country without a plan, right? Well, you shouldn't run your business without one either. A financial strategy takes everything we've discussed—cash flow, budgeting, forecasting—and pulls it all together into a plan that guides you toward your financial goals. It's about being proactive, not reactive, and making sure that every dollar you spend is moving your business in the right direction.

But here's the kicker: creating a strategy isn't just about numbers. It's about aligning your finances with your business goals. So, what are your long-term goals? Are you trying to increase revenue, reduce costs, or expand into new markets? Whatever it is, your financial strategy should be the tool that gets you there. So, let's dive into how to create one.

1. Set Clear Financial Goals

Before you start cranking out spreadsheets and tracking every penny, you need to know where you're going. Are you looking to increase profits by 20% over the next year? Maybe you want to cut your operating costs by 10%? Whatever your goals are, be specific. Without clear goals, your strategy is like setting out on a road trip without a destination—just driving in circles.

2. Know Your Cash Flow

You can't manage what you don't measure. Cash flow is the lifeblood of your business—if it's healthy, your business is healthy. You need to know exactly when cash is coming in, when it's going out, and what you're left with. Look at your revenue, your expenses, and the timing of it all. Are you going to have enough cash to cover next month's expenses? This is about keeping your business running without surprise roadblocks.

3. Create a Budget That Actually Works

A budget isn't just a list of numbers—it's a plan. Think of it like the blueprint for building a house. Your budget should be based on realistic expectations of income and expenses. Start by looking at past data (don't just guess), then figure out what you expect to make and where your money will go. Break it down into categories: operating costs, marketing, salaries, taxes, etc. And most importantly, track it. A budget is useless if it's just a piece of paper you never look at.

4. Forecast for the Future

Now that you know where you are, it's time to think about where you're going. Financial forecasting helps you predict future revenue and expenses based on your current situation. You want to create different scenarios—best case, worst case, and most likely case. That way, you're prepared for whatever happens and can adjust your plan if needed. Forecasting is a big-picture tool that helps keep your financial strategy aligned with your goals.

5. Manage Your Debt Wisely

If your business is carrying debt (which most do at some point), don't ignore it. Debt management should be part of your strategy. Create a plan to pay it down gradually while still maintaining cash flow for operations. If you're taking on new debt, make sure it's for something that'll move your business forward—like investing in equipment or expanding operations, not just covering short-term expenses.

6. Evaluate Your Profitability and Costs

Now, let's talk about the numbers behind your success. Are you making enough profit for the work you're putting in? If you're constantly feeling squeezed, it might be time to re-evaluate your pricing strategy or take a closer look at where you're spending. Can you reduce expenses without affecting quality? Is there room to increase your margins? This is about finding the sweet spot where revenue exceeds your costs, leaving you with healthy profits.

7. Build an Emergency Fund

Here's the thing: stuff happens. You can plan, forecast, and budget all you want, but unexpected costs will pop up. That's why having an emergency fund is non-negotiable. It's your financial cushion—designed to get you through rough patches without having to scramble for cash. Set aside a portion of your profits to build and maintain this fund. It's not about making it big; it's about staying afloat when the waters get choppy.

Common Pitfalls To Avoid

Let's get real for a second. Now that you've got the blueprint for creating a solid financial strategy, it's time to talk about the pitfalls. Because let's face it, no one ever really talks about the stuff that'll trip you up when it comes to managing money. The truth is, you can have the perfect plan in place, but if you're not aware of the common mistakes that will throw you off track, all that hard work can easily go down the drain.

So let's dive into the traps that even experienced business owners fall into, and how to avoid them like a pro. You don't want your strategy to be perfect in theory, only to watch it collapse because of avoidable mistakes. Here's where the rubber meets the road: keeping it simple, staying disciplined, and being mindful of these pitfalls will help you keep your finances on track.

1. Ignoring Cash Flow

Here's the deal: cash flow is king. Period. A lot of businesses dive headfirst into trying to scale, thinking that revenue is all that matters, but without cash flow management, it's like building a castle out of sand. Sure, you've got the looks, but the next wave's coming, and you're going down fast. Cash flow is what keeps the lights on, pays the bills, and keeps your employees happy. If you're not tracking it daily or weekly, you're asking for trouble. Monitor your inflows and outflows regularly and make sure you always have enough working capital to cover your basic operational expenses.

2. Overestimating Revenue

I get it, we're all optimists when we're in love with our business idea. But don't let that optimism cloud your judgment. Businesses often overestimate future revenue, thinking they're going to crush it in the first six months. Reality check: it takes time to build up customer loyalty, trust, and consistent revenue streams. Budget conservatively and plan for a slower ramp-up, not instant success. Be realistic with your projections, and don't rely on "what ifs." Keep your expectations in check.

3. Neglecting Profit Margins

Sure, revenue is exciting, but what about profit margins? Just because you're making money doesn't mean you're *making money*. If you're not tracking your margins—how much you're actually earning after costs—then you're likely spinning your wheels. A lot of businesses waste cash by overpricing or underpricing their products, not factoring in operational costs, or failing to streamline expenses. If you're not making enough per sale, you're just working harder for less.

4. Not Budgeting for Emergencies

You know that old saying, "Prepare for the worst, hope for the best"? It's not just for the military. In business, you need to budget for the unexpected. Emergencies—whether it's a machine breakdown, a marketing campaign flop, or a global pandemic—are going to happen. If you don't have an emergency fund or buffer in place, one bump in the road could send you off a cliff. Start setting aside a percentage of your earnings for unforeseen circumstances. Trust me, when the unexpected hits, you'll be glad you did.

5. Failing to Separate Personal and Business Finances

Look, I know it's tempting to dip into your business funds for that shiny new toy or a personal emergency, but don't do it. Mixing your personal finances with your business is a rookie mistake. Not only does it make things confusing, but it can also cause tax headaches and mess with your financial reports. Keep your business accounts separate from your personal ones and treat your business like a professional operation—not a piggy bank.

6. Not Reviewing Your Financials Regularly

If you're not reviewing your financials on a regular basis—like, at least once a month—you're just hoping for the best. Successful businesses are built on consistent monitoring and evaluation. When you review your financials, you can identify patterns, spot red flags early, and adjust your strategy. Don't wait until your bank balance is dry to check in. Make it a habit to look over your numbers and adjust your plans as needed.

7. Neglecting Taxes

Oh, taxes. The necessary evil of every business. But let me tell you this: ignore them at your own risk. If you're not setting aside enough for taxes throughout the year, you're setting yourself up for a big, ugly surprise come tax season. Make sure you're budgeting for both federal and state taxes, and don't try to play catch-up later. Hire a professional if you need to, but don't put off what you know is coming.

These pitfalls aren't here to scare you; they're here to keep you in check. Avoiding these mistakes is crucial for long-term success, and if you can do that, you'll have the financial foundation you need to scale. Remember, a solid financial strategy isn't just about making money—it's about keeping it, using it wisely, and having a plan to weather the inevitable storms. Keep your eyes on the prize, but don't let your finances go off-course because of preventable errors.

Final Thoughts

By following these steps, you're not just guessing your way through business finances—you're setting a clear strategy that aligns your financial goals with the practical steps to get there. It's about being smart with your money and staying proactive so you can make decisions with confidence. Now, with your financial strategy in place, you're ready to navigate the business world without running into a wall every time a new challenge comes up.

To close this chapter, let me remind you of something that most business owners forget: financial management isn't just about keeping the lights on. It's about making your money work for you, not the other way around. When you have a solid financial strategy in place, you're no longer reacting to cash flow crises or scrambling to cover costs. You're in control. You have a plan for today, tomorrow, and the future.

Building and managing a business is hard enough without throwing money problems into the mix. So, when you put in the work to create a financial strategy, you're setting yourself up for stability, growth, and the kind of long-term success that lets you step back from the grind and focus on what matters most—building the business you actually want.

So get real with your finances. Set those goals. Track the cash flow. Don't let your expenses run away from you. And always, always keep that emergency fund padded and ready. Once you've done the work, you'll find yourself less stressed and better prepared for whatever life throws at you—whether that's an economic downturn or just another crazy day of running your business.

With a solid financial strategy in place, you'll move from chaos to control—and that's a huge win for any business owner. Keep your eyes on the big picture, stick to the strategy, and get your business to where it needs to be, with plenty of runway to spare. Now, go forth and take charge of those numbers! The next chapter awaits, and it's time to move on to the next gear.

Let's Put This Into Action

Here's a simple prompt to help you kickstart your financial strategy:

"Help me create a financial strategy for my business. I want to define key areas like cash flow management, budgeting, revenue projections, profit margins, and tax planning. Guide me in setting realistic financial goals, forecasting future revenues, and ensuring I have a solid plan for both growth and unexpected emergencies. Make sure to break it down into actionable steps with clear metrics to track progress and identify potential risks."

This prompt will help you organize your financial game plan, setting a strong foundation to manage your money, grow your business, and avoid costly mistakes down the road. Keep it simple, keep it real, and get to work!

BLUE PHASE: GROWTH

☆★☆

Chapter 8:
MARKETING

When I first met my wife, I was in a phase where I knew exactly what I wanted. I wasn't just casually dating—I was looking for something real. So, on our very first date, I laid it all out there: *"I want to get married and have kids."*

Now, I *thought* I was being upfront and efficient. No games, no wasted time. But judging by the look on her face, I might as well have asked her to sign a 30-year mortgage with me right then and there.

This was not a good strategy. Asking for *that* level of commitment *that fast* didn't make her feel excited—it made her feel pressured. I was skipping the entire process of getting to know each other, of building trust, of making sure we actually *liked* spending time together before making any big decisions.

It took months of dates, conversations, and consistency before she was ready to take that next step. And today? We're married with two kids. And she *still* jokes with me (and all our friends) about how I nearly scared her off with my "marriage and kids" speech on date one.

The same goes for marketing.

Too many business owners make the *exact same* mistake with their marketing. They show up, get in front of a prospect for the first time, and immediately go for the sale:

- "Buy now!"
- "Sign up today!"
- "Let's book a call right now!"

It's the marketing equivalent of proposing on the first date.

But here's the thing—people don't buy from businesses they don't trust. Just like dating, customers need time to get to know you, understand what you offer, and decide whether you're the right fit for them.

Marketing, like relationships, happens in three stages:

1. **Hook (Attract & Get Their Attention)**

   - This is like that first date. You need to *capture their interest*—but not in a way that makes them run for the hills. Your job is to make a great first impression and get them to want to learn more.

   - In marketing, this could be a killer one-liner, a strong social media presence, or a well-placed ad that speaks directly to their problem.

2. Educate (Build Trust & Show Value)

- Once you've got their attention, you need to *keep showing up*. Just like I had to keep going on dates to show my wife I was serious, you have to consistently provide value to your audience.

- This might mean offering free resources (like a lead magnet), sending helpful emails, posting valuable content, or just engaging with them regularly.

3. Commitment (The Sale – But Only When They're Ready)

- If you've done the first two steps right, this part feels natural. By the time your prospect is ready to buy, they already trust you. They know what you offer, how it helps them, and why they should choose you.

- This is where you make the clear ask, whether that's booking a call, signing up for your service, or clicking "Buy Now."

So, are you proposing on the first date?

Think about your marketing right now—are you trying to rush people into a decision before they're ready? Are you hitting them with a sales pitch the moment they discover you?

Because if you are, you're scaring them off just like I almost did with my wife.

Instead, play the long game. Focus on attracting the right people, showing up consistently, and building trust. When you do that, by the time you make the ask, they'll already be thinking, *"Yeah, I'm ready for this."*

And that's how you *actually* close the deal.

So, what goes into good marketing?

If there's one thing I see over and over with small business owners, it's this: most of them have no idea how to market. Ask them what they're doing for marketing, and the answers are usually some variation of:

- "I post on social media every once in a while."

- "I tried ads once, but they didn't work."

- "I'm all word of mouth."

Let me be clear: word of mouth is not a marketing strategy. It's a nice bonus when it happens, but if that's your entire plan, you're basically relying on hope—and hope isn't a business strategy. And those random social media posts? That's not marketing either. That's like fishing with no bait and wondering why nothing's biting.

Marketing is the engine that drives business growth. Every time I work with a business that's struggling, it's almost always because their marketing is either nonexistent or completely random. But the second we crank up the marketing and do it right, everything starts falling into place—leads come in, sales go up, and suddenly the business isn't just surviving, it's thriving.

So, what separates good marketing from just throwing stuff out there and hoping for the best?

1. **It's Clear as Hell** – If people don't immediately understand what you do and why it matters to them, they'll move on. Your marketing message needs to pass the "grunt test"—as in, someone should be able to glance at it and instantly know who you help, how

you help them, and what they need to do next. No fluff. No jargon. Just straight to the point.

2. **It Speaks to a Specific Person** – If you try to market to everyone, you'll connect with no one. Good marketing is laser-focused on a specific customer—their pain points, their desires, their language. When your message makes someone think, "Damn, that's me," you've got them.

3. **It Makes an Offer They Actually Want** – The best marketing doesn't just *tell* people about your business; it gives them a reason to care. That means offering something compelling—whether it's solving a frustrating problem, saving them time or money, or giving them something they *need* but didn't even realize existed. If your offer isn't irresistible, your marketing won't work.

4. **It's Consistent** – The brands that win aren't always the loudest, but they are the most consistent. Good marketing isn't about one killer ad or a great campaign—it's about showing up again and again, so when someone *finally* needs what you offer, you're the first name that comes to mind.

5. **It Has a Clear Next Step** – People don't take action unless you tell them exactly what to do. A strong call to action (CTA) is non-negotiable. Whether it's "Call now," "Download this," or "Book a free consultation," you need to make it stupidly easy for people to move forward. If you're vague, they'll do nothing.

6. **It's Measurable and Repeatable** – If you can't track what's working, you can't improve it. Good marketing isn't about guessing—it's about testing, refining, and doubling down on what brings results.

The best businesses don't just "do marketing." They build systems that predictably generate leads and sales.

Marketing isn't optional. If you don't market, you don't grow. If you're relying on referrals and the occasional Facebook post, you're playing small and leaving money on the table. If you want a business that thrives—not just survives—you need a marketing system that works day in and day out.

Get this part right, and the rest of your business gets a whole lot easier.

How to Create a Marketing Strategy That Actually Works

We've already established that every prospect moves through the same three phases—Hook, Educate, and Commitment. But here's the thing: knowing that isn't enough. You need a system that actually puts those phases to work in your business. Because if you're just winging it—throwing out content, hoping people will eventually buy—you're leaving a lot of money on the table.

A great marketing strategy doesn't happen by accident. It's intentional. It guides people through the buying process, step by step, without confusion, friction, or wasted effort. That's what we're building here.

By the time we're done, you won't just *know* what a great marketing strategy looks like—you'll have a repeatable system that attracts the right people, moves them through the process, and turns them into paying customers.

Let's get to work.

Step 1: Answering the 4 Fundamental Questions

Before you throw money at ads, start posting on social media, or even print your first business card, you need to get crystal clear on four fundamental marketing questions. Without the answers, you're just throwing darts in the dark and hoping one lands.

Think of this as the foundation of your marketing strategy—if you get it wrong, everything else crumbles. If you get it right, every decision you make —ads, social media, website, content—becomes a strategic move rather than a guessing game.

Let's break them down one by one.

1. Who is (and is NOT) my target audience?

If your answer is "everyone", we've got a problem. Because if you're marketing to everyone, you're marketing to no one.

Your goal is to attract the right people and repel the wrong ones. The clearer you are about who you serve (and who you don't), the easier it is to create marketing that speaks directly to them.

Start by answering:

- What industry, demographic, or niche do I serve?

- What specific problems do they struggle with?

- What goals or desires are they chasing?

- What frustrations keep them up at night?

And just as importantly:

- Who is NOT my customer?

- Who do I NOT want to work with?

Example:

- A high-end landscaping company may target homeowners in upscale neighborhoods who value sustainability, but they do not serve bargain hunters looking for the cheapest lawn care.

- A business coach may target 6-figure entrepreneurs who want to scale, but not side hustlers looking for free advice.

Get specific. You don't need a huge audience—you need the right audience.

2. Where do they hang out?

Once you know who you're targeting, the next step is figuring out where they spend their time. Because if your ideal customers are on LinkedIn, but you're spending all your time on TikTok, you're wasting effort.

- Are they active on social media? If so, which platforms?

- Do they read blogs, trade magazines, or industry news sites?

- Do they listen to podcasts or watch YouTube videos?

- Are they part of networking groups, online communities, or local meetups?

- Do they attend specific conferences or events?

Your marketing needs to meet your audience where they already are—not where you wish they were.

Example:

- If you're targeting corporate professionals, focus on LinkedIn and industry blogs rather than Instagram.

- If you're a local gym, your audience is likely on Facebook, Instagram, and in community Facebook groups.

- If you sell luxury home services, you might reach your audience through high-end home magazines or referral networks.

Knowing where your people hang out means you can put your message in front of them when and where they're paying attention.

3. What do I want them to do?

This is where most businesses fail. They put out content, ads, or social posts without a clear call to action (CTA). If you don't tell people what to do next, they won't do anything.

Ask yourself:

- Do I want them to book a call?

- Do I want them to buy now?

- Do I want them to download a free resource?

- Do I want them to sign up for my newsletter?

- Do I want them to visit my website?

Be specific. If you're vague, your audience will scroll right past your message.

Bad CTA:

"Check out our services" - Too broad. No urgency. No clear action.

Good CTA:

"Book a free 15-minute strategy call now" - Clear action, low commitment, easy to follow.

Think of your CTA as the next step in the relationship. Make it obvious, make it easy, and make it valuable.

4. What Will I Say to Them? (Your One-Liner)

Your one-liner isn't just a cute tagline—it's your hook. It's the thing that grabs attention and makes people want to know more. If your message doesn't stop someone in their tracks and make them think, "Tell me more," then it's not doing its job.

Think of your one-liner as the first domino in your marketing. If it's strong, it leads people to the next step—visiting your website, asking a question, or downloading a resource. If it's weak, they'll move on, and you've lost them.

A great one-liner follows this simple structure:

"We help [target audience] solve [problem] by [solution] so they can [desired result]."

Here's how that looks in action:

- "We help small business owners systemize their operations so they can scale without working 24/7."

- "We provide home renovation services for busy professionals so they can enjoy a beautiful home without the hassle."

- "We help parents of picky eaters get their kids to love healthy foods—without mealtime battles."

Each of these statements does three things:

   a.   Gets attention by speaking directly to the person's pain point

   b.   Creates curiosity by making them want to learn more

   c.   Pushes them to the next step—whether that's asking a follow-up question, visiting a website, or signing up for something valuable

Your one-liner is the bait—it hooks people in. Once they're hooked, your website, lead magnet, and nurture campaigns educate them and move them toward commitment.

Test your one-liner in real conversations. If people respond with, "Oh, that's interesting—tell me more," you've nailed it. If they just nod and move on, go back to the drawing board.

Once you have a killer one-liner, everything else in your marketing becomes easier—because now, you've got people leaning in instead of tuning out.

Step 2: Building a Website That Converts

Your website isn't just an online business card—it's your 24/7 salesperson. It's where all your marketing efforts should point because this is the place where people can actually do something that makes you money. They can buy, book a call, sign up, or take the next step toward becoming a customer.

The mistake most businesses make? They treat their website like a brochure instead of a sales tool. If someone lands on your site and isn't sure what you do or what they should do next, they'll click away faster than a bad Tinder date. You have seconds to hook them.

A high-converting website should follow the same relationship flow:

    a.   Hook: Grab attention immediately.

    b.   Educate: Explain what you do and why it matters.

    c.   Commitment: Make it easy for them to take action.

Let's break that down:

1. Hook Them Immediately (Above the Fold)

"Above the fold" is the first thing people see on your website before they scroll. This section needs to hook them fast by answering three things:

- What do you do?

- Who is it for?

- How does it help them?

This is where your one-liner from Step 1 should go. Big, bold, and clear. No fluff. No corporate jargon. No "Welcome to our website" nonsense.

Then, right underneath that—your call to action (CTA). This is the most important button on your website. Make it clear and direct:

"Book a Free Consultation"

"Start Your Free Trial"

"Download the Guide"

A weak CTA is something vague like "Learn More" or "Contact Us." Nobody's excited to "learn more." They need clear direction on the next step.

2. Educate Them (The Middle of the Page)

Once they're hooked, now you need to build trust and explain why they should care. This section is your chance to educate them on what makes your business different and why your solution is what they need.

Here's what should be in this section:

a. The Problem You Solve: Speak to their pain points so they feel understood.

b. Your Unique Solution: Explain how your business solves their problem.

c. Proof: Use testimonials, case studies, or results to back up your claims.

d. A Simple Process: Show them the step-by-step of what happens when they work with you.

Example layout:

- Struggling to keep up with your business operations? You're not alone. Most business owners spend more time working in their business than on it. That's where we come in.

- Our Solution? We create automated systems that handle your operations so you can focus on growth.

- How It Works: (1) Book a free strategy call, (2) We assess your business, (3) You get a step-by-step automation plan.

- Join hundreds of business owners who've scaled stress-free.

Use simple, direct language that speaks to your audience. No fluff. No tech jargon. The goal here is to educate without overwhelming.

3. Get the Commitment (Call to Action & Lead Magnet)

Now that you've hooked them and educated them, it's time to ask for the commitment.

But here's the thing—not everyone is ready to buy immediately. Some people need more time. This is why your website should have two CTAs:

a. The Buy Now CTA (for those who are ready to commit)

b. The Lead Magnet CTA (for those who need more nurturing)

Example:

"Book a Free Strategy Call" (Primary CTA for buyers)

"Download Our Free Scaling Cheat Sheet" (For those who aren't ready but want value)

Your lead magnet keeps prospects engaged with your brand until they're ready to buy. It could be a free guide, checklist, or video training—anything valuable that solves a small part of their problem. Once they download it, you can continue nurturing them through email marketing.

Remember—every marketing effort you do should drive people to this website.

Social media posts, networking, ads, everything—it all leads back here, where they can actually take action.

Step 3: Capture Leads with a Lead Magnet

Not everyone who lands on your website is ready to pull the trigger and buy today—but that doesn't mean they're a lost cause. Most people need time before making a purchase decision, and if you're not staying in front of them, they'll forget you exist. That's where a lead magnet comes in.

Why Use a Lead Magnet?

A lead magnet is something valuable you give away for free in exchange for an email address. It's not just some random freebie—it's a tool that builds trust, keeps you top of mind, and moves people further down your sales funnel.

Think of it like this: If someone walks into a store and browses but doesn't buy anything, they leave and likely never come back. But if the store owner offers them a free sample in exchange for their contact info, they now have a direct way to remind them why they stopped by in the first place.

A good lead magnet gives your potential customers a quick win. It helps them solve a small piece of their problem while positioning you as the expert who can help them solve the whole thing.

What Makes a Good Lead Magnet?

- It solves a specific problem. It's not just "nice-to-have" content—it should be something your ideal customer actually wants.

- It's quick and easy to consume. No one wants a 100-page eBook. Think checklists, templates, mini-guides, or quick training videos.

- It naturally leads to your paid offer. Your lead magnet should be relevant to what you sell so that when they're ready to buy, you're the obvious choice.

How a Lead Magnet Fits Into Your Sales Funnel

Once someone downloads your lead magnet, they're not just a random visitor anymore—they're now a lead. That means you own their contact information and can follow up with them through email marketing.

Here's how it works:

a. They enter their email to get your lead magnet.

b. Their email is added to your CRM (Customer Relationship Management system).

c. They get put on a drip campaign—**a series of automated emails that keep them engaged, educate them about your solution, and nurture them toward a buying decision.

d. When the timing is right, they buy.

A good drip campaign doesn't just spam people with sales pitches—it educates, adds value, and builds trust. It keeps you in their inbox so that when they finally hit the point where they need your product or service, you're the first name that comes to mind.

Lead Magnet + CRM + Drip Campaign = A Sales Machine

Your website shouldn't just be a digital business card—it should be a lead-generating machine. A lead magnet helps capture visitors who aren't ready to buy today so you can nurture them into buyers later.

Step 4: Building Sales and Nurture Campaigns

Alright, so you've got a website that converts, and you've set up a lead magnet that brings potential customers into your world. Now, it's time to turn those leads into paying customers.

This is where email marketing comes in. But not just any emails— we're talking strategic sales and nurture campaigns that guide prospects toward making a buying decision.

The Two Types of Email Campaigns You Need

There are two key email campaigns that every business needs:

1. Sales Campaign (Immediate Follow-Up to the Lead Magnet)

2. Nurture Campaign (For People Who Aren't Ready to Buy Yet)

Let's break these down.

1. The Sales Campaign: Strike While the Iron's Hot

When someone downloads your lead magnet, that's your window of opportunity. They've raised their hand and said, "Hey, I'm interested in what you're talking about." Now, it's time to help them take the next step toward buying.

A sales campaign is a short, focused sequence of emails that encourages them to make a purchase, schedule a call, or take some other direct action that leads to revenue.

Sales Campaign Formula (3-5 Emails)

- Email 1 (Right After Download): "Here's your [Lead Magnet] + Quick Win" – Keep it simple. Give them the resource they requested, reinforce why it's valuable, and introduce how your product/service can help.

- Email 2 (The Next Day): "The Real Problem You're Facing" – Dig into the deeper issue they're dealing with and show them how your solution solves it.

- Email 3 (Social Proof & Success Stories): "How [Other Clients] Got Results" – Share testimonials, case studies, or personal success stories.

- Email 4 (Overcoming Objections): "You Might Be Thinking..." – Address common doubts or concerns they might have about buying from you.

- Email 5 (Final Call to Action): "Last Chance to [Take Action]" – Create urgency and encourage them to act now.

These emails should feel helpful, not pushy. You're showing them why your solution makes sense—not forcing them into anything.

Bonus

Because I know that building a high-converting sales campaign from scratch can feel overwhelming, I've put together a free sales campaign outline to help you get started.

This outline will show you:

a. The exact sequence of emails and touchpoints you need to move prospects through the buying journey.

b. How to craft a persuasive message that speaks directly to your audience's needs and objections.

c. When to follow up (and how often) so you stay top-of-mind without annoying people.

d. A simple call-to-action strategy that makes it easy for people to say "yes" to working with you.

Grab Your Free Sales Campaign Outline Now

Head over to https://tgscoaching.com/resources/ and download your free copy of the Sales Campaign Outline.

If typing a link isn't your thing, just scan the QR code below and get instant access.

This is the same framework I use to help businesses close more deals and grow faster—so don't skip it.

Marketing brings people in, but your sales campaign is what actually gets them to buy. Make sure you have a system in place that does the heavy lifting for you. Download the outline now and start closing more deals today!

2. The Nurture Campaign: Staying Top of Mind

Not everyone will buy right away—and that's completely normal. This is where most business owners give up. They think, "Well, they didn't buy, so I guess they're not interested."

Wrong.

They're just not ready—yet. And your job is to stay in front of them until they are.

This is where your nurture campaign comes in. If they don't buy after the sales campaign, they move into a longer-term email sequence that keeps them engaged, educates them, and reminds them you exist without being annoying.

What Goes into a Nurture Campaign?

- Educational Content – Share industry insights, common mistakes to avoid, or tips related to your business.

- Personal Stories – People connect with stories, not just information. Share your journey, lessons learned, or case studies of past clients.

- Success Stories & Testimonials – Keep showing proof that your product/service delivers results.

- Occasional Offers – Maybe they weren't ready before, but that doesn't mean they won't be now. Give them another chance.

How Often Should You Send Emails?

- First few weeks: Every 3-5 days

- Long-term: Once per week or twice per month

"I Don't Want to Spam People" (Let's Talk About That)

A lot of business owners hesitate when it comes to email marketing because they don't want to annoy their audience.

Here's the truth:

- Most people won't even read every email you send. But when they finally need what you offer, you'll be there.

- Email laws require an easy unsubscribe button. If they don't want your emails, they can (and will) opt out. That's fine— focus on those who stay.

- The biggest mistake isn't sending too many emails—it's not sending enough. If you don't stay top of mind, your competitors will.

Think about the emails you get from brands you like. Maybe you don't open them all, but when you're ready to buy, you know exactly where to go. That's the goal here.

Common Pitfalls to Avoid

If you're going to put in the effort, you need to make sure you're avoiding the most common marketing mistakes. Otherwise, you're just spinning your wheels and burning cash. Let's break down the biggest pitfalls that will tank your marketing efforts—and how to fix them.

1. Talking to Everyone (AKA Talking to No One)

The Mistake:

Trying to market to "everyone" is the fastest way to make sure your message resonates with no one. If your audience is too broad, your messaging will be watered down, and people won't feel like you're speaking directly to them.

The Fix:

Narrow it down. Get laser-focused on your ideal customer—who they are, what they struggle with, what they want. If you haven't done this yet, go back to Step 1 and dial in your one-liner. When you know who you're talking to, your marketing will be 100x more effective.

2. No Clear Call to Action

The Mistake:

Your website, social media, or ads are getting attention, but nobody's buying. Why? Because you're not telling them exactly what to do next. If your audience has to guess what the next step is, they won't take it.

The Fix:

Every single piece of marketing should have a clear, direct call to action (CTA). "Schedule a call," "Download the guide," "Buy now"—make it obvious, make it easy, and put it everywhere. If someone lands on your website and has to "figure out" how to buy from you, you've already lost them.

3. Driving Traffic to Nowhere

The Mistake:

You're posting on social media, running ads, attending networking events—but where are you sending people? If all roads don't lead back to your website (where they can actually do business with you), you're wasting your time.

The Fix:

Your website is the hub of your business. Everything—from social posts to ads to conversations at events—should push people to your website. And once they're there, make sure they have two options:

- Buy now (or book a call)

- Download a lead magnet (so you can nurture them until they're ready)

Your website shouldn't just look pretty—it should be built to convert.

4. No Lead Magnet (Missing Out on Future Customers)

The Mistake:

Not everyone is ready to buy the first time they hear about you. If you don't capture their information, they'll forget about you and move on. That's why relying only on word-of-mouth or "hope marketing" is a losing game.

The Fix:

Create a lead magnet—something valuable that solves a problem for your audience in exchange for their email address. Once they're on your list, put them on a nurture campaign so you stay top of mind. This way, when they're ready to buy, you're the first person they think of.

5. Ignoring Follow-Up (Because You "Don't Want to Spam People")

The Mistake:

A lot of business owners are afraid to follow up. They think they'll annoy people or come across as pushy. But here's the truth: most people won't even see your first message—and even if they do, they're busy. It takes multiple touchpoints to get someone to take action.

The Fix:

Set up a sales and nurture email campaign. If someone joins your email list but doesn't buy right away, don't just let them sit there—stay in front of them with useful content, success stories, and occasional offers. And don't worry about spamming—as long as your emails are helpful and relevant, they'll appreciate them. Plus, there's an unsubscribe button if they're not interested.

6. Inconsistent Marketing Efforts (AKA "Feast or Famine" Syndrome)

The Mistake:

Some business owners go all in on marketing when things are slow, then ghost their audience when they get busy. This leads to the classic "feast or famine" cycle—one month you have more clients than you can handle, the next month you're wondering where they all went.

The Fix:

Consistency wins. Whether it's social media, email marketing, or ads, you need a system in place that keeps your marketing running even when you're busy. Automate your emails, schedule your social posts in advance, and make sure your website is always working for you.

7. Thinking Marketing is a "One-and-Done" Task

The Mistake:

Marketing isn't something you "set and forget." It's not a box you check off once and call it a day. It's an ongoing process.

The Fix:

Track your results, analyze what's working, and keep improving. Marketing changes—platforms update, customer preferences shift, and new trends emerge. Stay agile, pay attention to the data, and adjust your strategy as needed.

Final Thoughts

Imagine this: You're at a networking event, talking to someone who fits your ideal client profile. The conversation is flowing, they seem interested in what you do, and then—boom—the moment of truth. They ask, "So, how can I learn more?"

What do you say?

Do you fumble through a half-baked explanation? Do you tell them to "follow you on Instagram" and hope they remember? Do you hand them a business card and pray they don't lose it in their junk drawer?

Or do you confidently point them to a website that guides them step-by-step from curiosity to commitment?

That's the difference between scattered marketing and a real strategy that works.

Marketing is just a giant funnel leading to one place—your website. Every action you take—whether it's posting on social media, attending a networking event, running an ad, or sending an email—is just another doorway leading people toward a place where they can actually take action.

Why? Because your website is where business happens.

- It's where people book a call.

- It's where they buy a product.

- It's where they sign up for your lead magnet (so you can stay top of mind).

- It's where they learn about your services and make a decision.

If your marketing isn't guiding people toward a next step on your website, then you're just making noise.

The biggest mistake business owners make? They market without direction.

- They post on Instagram because they feel like they "should."

- They show up to networking events without a follow-up plan.

- They run ads that lead to... nowhere.

Marketing without a strategy is like filling up a bucket full of holes—it doesn't matter how much effort you pour in, you're still leaking leads.

That's why every single thing you do needs to connect to a system that brings people from hook to education to commitment.

- That Facebook ad? It shouldn't just be a cool post—it should send them to a landing page where they can book a call.

- That Instagram reel? It should have a clear CTA leading to your website, where they can sign up for something valuable.

- That networking conversation? It shouldn't end with "let's stay in touch." It should end with, "Here's where you can get my free guide—check it out."

Everything should have one goal—get them to your website so they can take action.

If you've been following along, you now have a complete system for marketing:

Step 1: Hook them with a one-liner that grabs their attention.

Step 2: Drive them to a website that educates and converts.

Step 3: Capture leads with a valuable lead magnet.

Step 4: Follow up with sales and nurture campaigns to close the deal.

Now, every touchpoint you create feeds into this system. No more wasted efforts. No more hoping people "just remember" to come back.

Instead, your marketing becomes a well-oiled machine—one that brings in leads, nurtures them, and turns them into paying customers.

If your marketing doesn't have a next step, it's a dead end. And dead ends don't make sales.

So, from here on out, make a promise to yourself: Every piece of marketing you put into the world should drive people toward your website. Because that's where they can buy, book, or sign up. That's where business actually happens.

Now, go put your system to work.

Let's Put This Into Action

A.I. supercharges your Growth by deepening customer connections and pinpointing opportunities. Tools like HubSpot or Salesforce use A.I. to analyze customer behavior—say, identifying which clients are most likely to reorder based on past purchases. A retail owner might use A.I. to craft personalized email campaigns, boosting repeat sales by 20%. Or, use a tool like Google Analytics' predictive metrics to spot which products are trending, so you can double down on marketing them. Check the A.I. prompt at the end of this chapter to draft your marketing strategy and use A.I. to map your customer data and uncover growth levers you've been missing.

Prompt:

"I run a [TYPE OF BUSINESS] that specializes in [PRODUCT/SERVICE]. My ideal customers are [DESCRIBE TARGET AUDIENCE: who they are, what they struggle with, what they desire]. I want them to [DESIRED ACTION: book a call, buy a product, sign up for a free resource, etc.]. My brand message needs to clearly communicate [ONE-LINER: what problem I solve, for whom, how, and the results they'll get].

I need a marketing strategy that follows a Hook, Educate, and Commitment framework, driving traffic to my website where prospects can either purchase immediately or download a lead magnet in exchange for their email.

The strategy should include:

1. A clear one-liner that instantly grabs attention and explains what I do.

2. Website recommendations that improve conversions and clearly guide visitors toward action.

3. Lead magnet ideas that would appeal to my target audience and increase email sign-ups.

4. Sales and nurture email campaign outlines, including what to send and when.

5. The best marketing channels to reach my audience (social media, SEO, paid ads, networking, etc.).

6. A structured marketing plan that ensures consistent engagement and follow-ups.

7. Based on my customer data [describe your data], what products or services are likely to drive repeat sales?

Please provide a detailed plan that is easy to implement and tailored to my business. Use the results to target my Growth efforts."

☆☆☆

Chapter 9:
SALES

Let me take you back to when I was a high school senior with absolutely no plan for my future—other than, throwing the best parties and being the class clown. I wasn't exactly top of my class. In fact, if my grades were any lower, you'd need a mining helmet and a pickaxe to find them. The SATs? Don't even get me started. I filled in random bubbles on the answer sheet just so I could get the rest of the day off. When it came time to sit down with my guidance counselor and I had 15 minutes to determine my future, I wasn't prepared. Not even close.

I told him I wanted to go to college, but let's be real—I only wanted to go because I heard college had way better parties than high school. So, when my counselor looked at my SAT scores, and my grades, he stared at them for a second, then looked up at me like I'd just told him I planned to become an astronaut. He shook his head and said, "Son, college isn't really in your future, but I do have a cousin who could use some help in the sanitation industry."

I blinked. "Sanitation?" I said, confused.

He dropped the bomb: "You'll be driving a truck with a giant vacuum and sucking shit out of porta-potties at public events."

I kid you not. This man—this supposed professional—was offering me a job that I wouldn't even give to my worst enemy. I wanted college. I wanted parties. And instead, he was offering me the glamorous life of a *shit sucker*. I walked out of that meeting like, "Well, guess I'll just figure it out later," but deep down I was like, "I can't be the guy driving the shit truck."

Flash forward to after graduation. I'm still living my best life, hanging out with my buddies, pumping gas at a full-service station, getting paid minimum wage. Meanwhile, all my friends were off doing *adult things*—getting real jobs, going to college, getting their shit together. It was a tough pill to swallow. And that's when I ran into an old friend at the mall who mentioned he was heading to talk to a military recruiter. I thought, "What the hell, I've got nothing else going on," and decided to tag along.

We roll up to this military recruiting station that has all branches under one roof. It's like a buffet of options.

I walked into the Air Force office first, all pumped up, and asked the recruiter, "Hey, do you guys like to party, and will you pay for college?"

The guy looks at me like I was his child and just told him I know how babies are made. He didn't even blink—just gave me this polite, pitying smile and said, "We're here to talk about career options, but if you're worried about partying, maybe the Air Force isn't for you."

Yeah, no kidding. I was expecting him to hand me a cocktail and a jet pilot suit, but apparently, they take things a little more seriously.

Off to the Navy. I walk in, same question. "Do you guys like to party? And will you pay for my college?"

He didn't skip a beat. He just launched into this well-rehearsed pitch about spending months on a boat traveling the world. And I'm sitting there thinking, "Alright, I can handle a boat. Maybe a little tropical island action, get some sun, it'd be like a cruise ship" So I asked, "But you can party on the boat, right?"

He looks at me, all serious, and says, "No, there are strict no alcohol policies while at sea"

I paused, took a second to process, and then said, "Wait, so no party, and it's a boat full of dudes?"

He just nodded. And I'm like, "Yeah, I'll pass."

Finally, I wander into the Army office. I ask the same question, "Do you guys like to party? And will you pay for my college?"

This recruiter—oh man—he didn't hesitate. He flashed a smile that could've sold ice to an Eskimo. He said, "Hell yeah, we like to party! And not only will we pay for your college, but we'll also pay *you* to go to college."

I'm sitting there like, "Sold." The guy literally mirrored my energy, understood exactly what I wanted—parties and a free ride—and he pitched it right to me.

At that moment, I was *in*. My mind was made up. I didn't even need to hear the rest of the pitch. Less than a month later, I'm off to basic training, ready to live my best life... or so I thought.

Here's the thing my recruiter understood: he listened. He didn't try to shove some generic pitch down my throat. He listened to what I *wanted*—I was a 18-year-old kid who wanted a good time and some direction. And that's exactly what he gave me. It wasn't pretty, and it wasn't exactly what I expected, but damn if it didn't work. I went in thinking I was getting college and parties, and while the parties were... *different*, I ended up with everything I needed, plus a free ride to college.

That's the power of sales. It's not just about pitching a product—it's about listening. It's about understanding what someone needs, what they want, and offering them the solution. That recruiter sold me not just a career but a dream. And whether you're selling a product or a service, that's what you've got to do: listen, match your solution to their needs, and make it clear how it will solve their problems. That's how you sell—by understanding what they *actually* want and making sure your offering matches it. And, just like that Army recruiter, when you get it right, you close the deal without them even knowing what hit 'em.

So, what goes into good sales?

Alright, now that I've given you a little glimpse into how a recruiter used a masterful sales pitch to sell me on the Army, let's talk about what makes good sales, because I've learned a thing or two about it since then.

You see, good sales isn't about trying to shove a product or service down someone's throat. It's about understanding what the person *actually* wants and then showing them how what you're offering can solve their problem or give them what they're looking for. It's about building rapport, asking the right questions, and tailoring your message in a way that makes them say, "Oh damn, that's exactly what I need!"

The Army recruiter didn't spend his time selling me on the harsh realities of military life—he didn't mention boot camp or the risk of death (and trust me, I wasn't thinking about that part). No, he was smart enough to focus on *what I wanted*—the college parties, the pay, the adventure. He was a pro at understanding me, at matching my energy, and getting me excited about what he was selling.

In other words, he didn't try to fit me into his sales pitch—he molded the pitch to fit *me*. And that's exactly what makes great sales. You've got to meet your prospect where they're at, and then walk them through how your solution can make their life better. If you've got that, you're on the right track.

Now, let's break it down into the ingredients that make good sales, so you can stop banging your head against the wall trying to convince people to buy something they don't want.

1. Understanding the Prospect

Before you start talking, you need to *listen* and really understand who you're talking to. This is the foundation of great sales. It's not about you or your product—it's about *them*. What are their challenges? What do they want? What are they struggling with? If you're not asking the right questions and understanding the prospect's situation, you're just talking into the wind.

The Army recruiter? He didn't start by ramming information down my throat. He let me tell him what I wanted. He listened, and he focused on how his solution could fit *my* needs. Now, that's understanding your audience.

2. Building Rapport

Nobody buys from someone they don't trust or feel comfortable with. It's that simple. You've got to make a connection. People buy from people they like. Whether you're selling a service or a product, the first step is building rapport. Find common ground, share a laugh, and get them to relax. When you're at ease, it's easier for them to see you as someone who can help, not just a salesperson trying to make a commission.

My Army recruiter did this by matching my energy. I wasn't looking for a formal, stiff conversation. I wanted to *party*, and he gave me that vibe. He matched my humor, he understood where I was coming from, and boom—trust was built right there.

3. Presenting the Right Solution

Now that you've connected and understood what they're looking for, it's time to present the solution—but don't just toss everything at them. Focus on *what they care about* and show them exactly how your product or service solves their problem. Be clear, concise, and focus on the benefits that matter most to them.

The Army recruiter didn't give me some long spiel about the military structure or enlistment bonuses. He sold me on the parties, the college, and the pay. He didn't waste time with irrelevant details. He spoke my language, and that's what made the offer so attractive.

4. Handling Objections

Let's face it—there's always a moment when the prospect hesitates. Maybe it's price, maybe it's timing, or maybe they're just not sure. Handling objections isn't about getting defensive. It's about understanding *why* they're hesitant and providing a clear, logical reason to move forward.

When I asked about partying in the Navy, the recruiter didn't get all defensive or start arguing with me. He laid it out plainly—"No party, a bunch of dudes, and months on a boat." He acknowledged my concern and let me make the decision. If he'd started pushing back hard, it would've killed any chance of me buying in.

5. Creating Urgency

People don't act unless they feel they have to. That's just human nature. So, you need to create a sense of urgency. Not by being pushy, but by pointing out why taking action now makes sense. Whether it's a limited-time offer, a solution to an immediate problem, or an opportunity they can't pass up, urgency pushes them to act before they start overthinking and backing out.

The recruiter didn't spend a ton of time here, but he made it clear that if I didn't act soon, I'd miss out on the opportunity to earn a signing bonus. That urgency—without being overbearing—kept me moving forward.

6. Closing the Deal

The final part of sales is closing the deal. After all your work, the relationship, the trust, the handling of objections, and the solution you've offered, now you need to ask for the sale. Not in a desperate, sleazy way, but confidently and clearly. It's not about begging or twisting their arm. It's about making it easy for them to say yes.

In my case, the Army recruiter didn't ask me twice. He made the offer, answered my questions, and then handed me the paperwork. No pressure, just confidence. And that's how you close a deal—by making it clear, straightforward, and easy for the customer to say, "Let's do it."

There you have it—the basics of good sales. It's not rocket science, but it's a science all the same. Understand your prospect, build rapport, present a solution that fits, handle objections, create urgency, and close the deal. Simple as that.

Now, let's take these principles and apply them to your own sales process. Because if you're not doing these things, you're just wasting everyone's time—including your own.

How to create a sales process?

Alright, let's get into the meat and potatoes of this thing—creating your own sales process. Here's the deal: successful companies don't just wing it when it comes to sales. They don't rely on the luck of the draw or hope that the right words magically come out of the salesperson's mouth. Nope. They have a documented, step-by-step sales process. It's like the Army: rigid enough to keep you on track, but flexible enough to let you adapt to the mission at hand.

Think about it: you could be selling anything, from cupcakes to complex software, and if you're running a business, you better believe you need a game plan. This process isn't about turning your salespeople into robots who follow a script like some mindless drone. No, it's about giving them a framework—a proven process they can rely on that guides them through each conversation while still allowing room to adjust to the unique needs of each customer. That's how you make sure your team doesn't go off the rails but still keeps their personality and adaptability intact.

When you're building your own sales process, you've got to create something that works for your business. Something repeatable. You can't have your salespeople improvising every time they walk into a room. That's like throwing a party and hoping the right guests show up without actually inviting anyone—good luck with that.

But you also can't build a sales process so rigid that it feels like a scripted, one-size-fits-all nonsense. People can smell that stuff from a mile away. They want to feel like they're being heard, not like they're in a transaction. Your sales process needs to be a balance: structure to guide the conversation, flexibility to adjust, and a solid ending where the deal gets done.

So, let's break down how to create a sales process that's going to make sure your sales team is operating at their best—closing deals and building relationships like pros.

1. Lead Generation: Get 'Em in the Door

The first step of your sales process is making sure you've got leads coming in. This is where you build the foundation. You've got to know how you're finding these prospects. Whether it's through cold calls, social media, referrals, or some other method, you need a system for consistently bringing in potential customers who might be interested in what you've got to offer.

Think of this like setting the bait. You've got to know where to cast your line, what kind of bait works for your fish, and how often you need to cast it to fill your net. If you don't have leads, the rest of the process doesn't even matter.

2. Qualification: Not Every Lead Is a Winner

Once you've got your leads, you need to qualify them. This step is about figuring out which leads are really worth your time. Not everyone who shows up is going to be the right fit, and that's okay. The goal here is to assess whether the lead has the potential to become a customer. Are they the right size, in the right industry, and have the right need?

This is where you stop wasting time chasing down rabbits that aren't worth catching. Focus your efforts on the leads that actually have a chance of closing. You don't need every lead—you need the right ones.

3. Engagement: Building Trust and Finding Pain Points

This is where your sales process gets fun. It's not about just "selling" them on something. You've got to build rapport. Ask questions.

Listen. Find out what their problems are and how your product or service can solve them. The goal is to start a conversation, not just push a product.

When you're engaging with the prospect, think of it like you're having a good conversation at a bar (if you're not trying to close a deal while doing shots, that is). You've got to listen carefully to what they're saying and ask thoughtful follow-up questions. This isn't about delivering a rehearsed pitch; it's about letting them talk and showing you understand their pain.

4. Presentation: Show 'Em What You Got

Now that you've built some trust and discovered their needs, it's time to show them how your product or service is the answer to their problem. The presentation isn't about reading a script—it's about customizing your pitch to align with the issues they've shared with you.

This part is like showing someone your shiny new car, but instead of just saying "it's the best car," you point out how it has the exact features they need. You tell them how your product or service will make their life easier, save them money, or solve the problems they've been complaining about. Don't just talk at them—show them the benefits.

5. Handling Objections: Don't Let 'Em Slip Away

Now comes the fun part—objections. Guess what? If you're doing this right, they're gonna happen. And when they do, don't panic. This is where your sales skills really come into play. You're going to get "It's too expensive" or "I need to think about it." That's normal. What matters is how you handle it.

Don't push back too hard. You need to empathize, acknowledge their concern, and address it head-on. If they say it's too expensive, don't go into a rant about how cheap your product is—show them why it's worth the price and how it solves their problems better than anyone else.

6. Closing the Deal: Getting Them to Say 'Yes'

You've built rapport, you've listened to their needs, and you've addressed their concerns. Now it's time to close. But closing isn't about twisting their arm. It's about making it easy for them to say "yes." Offer options, create urgency, and make them feel like they're making the right decision.

This isn't a high-pressure, slick salesman move. It's about gently guiding them to the right decision. Maybe it's offering a discount for acting quickly or a special deal if they sign today. Whatever it is, make sure the next step is obvious and easy.

7. Follow-Up: Don't Let 'Em Forget You

Just because they signed the contract doesn't mean the work is done. Follow up, check in, and make sure they're happy with the decision they made. Not only does this ensure customer satisfaction, but it also sets you up for future opportunities, referrals, or even a bigger sale down the line.

This is about building a long-term relationship, not just a one-time transaction. Keep in touch, check on their needs, and show them that you're there to help, even after the deal is closed.

So, there you have it—a step-by-step guide for creating your sales process. It's got structure, but there's enough flexibility to let your team tweak it depending on the situation. After all, not every prospect is the same, but with a solid process in place, your team will have the confidence to know what to do next—and make more sales in the process.

Common Pitfalls To Avoid

Alright, so you've got your shiny new sales process all mapped out. You're ready to crush it. But before you start popping champagne and celebrating your new sales empire, let's talk about the common pitfalls that'll trip you up faster than a rookie trying to sell a paperclip to a minimalist.

Here's the truth: even the best sales process in the world can be derailed by a few classic mistakes. If you don't watch out, you'll end up wasting time, burning leads, and feeling like you're stuck in a perpetual cycle of "almosts" instead of "yeses." And believe me, those "almosts" are the kind of thing that'll make you want to punch a wall. So, let's dive into what to avoid, and save you from falling into these traps like a rookie.

1. Skipping the Discovery Phase

Look, I get it—you're excited to make the sale, you want the commission, and you want it now. But if you skip the discovery phase—the part where you ask questions, listen, and really understand the customer's needs—you're setting yourself up for failure. You can't just launch into your pitch like it's a one-size-fits-all. That's like showing up to a potluck with a bowl of cereal when everyone else is bringing steak and mashed potatoes. It doesn't work.

Not asking the right questions or diving into their specific pain points will make you sound like a used car salesman on a bad day. The key here? Slow down, and really get to know what they need before you start pitching. Trust me, you'll be a lot more successful.

2. Overloading with Features, Not Benefits

I've seen this too many times. Salespeople, especially new ones, love to rattle off every feature of their product like it's the greatest thing since sliced bread. "It has 15 settings, a touch screen, it can make coffee and save you the day after tomorrow!" But the customer? They don't care. They want to know *what's in it for them*. "Will this save me time? Will it make my life easier? Can it make me look like a superhero while I'm handling my workload?"

Stop talking about how cool your product is and start explaining how it solves *their* problem. Focus on the benefits. Let them see how your product is going to make their life better. If you don't, you'll just sound like a robot reciting specs—and nobody buys from robots.

3. Being Afraid to Close the Deal

This one's a killer. You've spent all this time nurturing the lead, listening to their problems, offering solutions—and then you just freeze. The dreaded moment comes when it's time to ask for the sale, and suddenly your tongue's tied like a rookie at prom. You start with the weak "Um, so would you maybe want to, uh, give this a try?" Big mistake.

Look, if you've done the work, if you've made the case, and you know your product's a good fit, then **ask for the damn sale**. Don't beat around the bush. Be confident, direct, and professional. "Are you ready to move forward with this today?" It's not rocket science, and no, it's not pushy if you've built trust and have given them a solid reason to buy. Just do it.

4. Neglecting Follow-Up

If you're not following up after your first conversation, you're basically throwing away all your hard work. A lead might not be ready to buy immediately, and that's fine. But if you don't follow up? Well, good luck. It's like doing all the prep work for a big meal and then forgetting to turn on the stove.

Sales aren't won on the first call 99% of the time. You've got to stay in the game. Whether it's a quick check-in email, a call to see how they're feeling, or sending them some relevant content, don't just drop the ball after one conversation. Follow up, be persistent (but not annoying), and stay top of mind.

5. Lack of Adaptability

Now, I get it. You've got a sales process and you're sticking to it like a soldier with a mission. But listen—if you're rigid to the point of ignoring what the customer is telling you, you're dead in the water. Sales is a dance, not a script. If the customer is giving you signs that they need something different, *adapt*. If you're still pushing the same spiel after they've shown you they're not buying it, you're just wasting both of your time.

Pay attention to their signals—emotional and verbal. If they're asking for more specifics, give it to them. If they're getting uneasy, switch gears. The key to success? Flexibility, baby. Know when to go off-script.

6. Not Tracking Your Results

If you're not measuring your performance, then what are you doing? You can't improve if you don't know where you're screwing up. You might be winging it, closing deals left and right, but if you're not tracking which steps in your sales process are working and which aren't, you'll never optimize.

You need data. Look at the numbers, track your conversions, understand your win rates, and see where leads are falling off. If you're not tracking, you're flying blind. It's that simple.

7. Ignoring the Power of Referrals

Let me make this clear—if you're not asking for referrals, you're a fool. Sales aren't just about closing deals with the people you're talking to right now. The best clients often come from referrals. You've done the hard work of building trust with a client—why not ask them to refer you to others?

But don't just ask like a beggar. Ask confidently. "I've really enjoyed working with you. If you know anyone who could use our services, I'd be honored to help them, too." Simple. Polite. Direct. And if they're happy with you, they'll pass you along. Salespeople who don't ask for referrals are the same people who forget to check their six. Big mistake.

So there you have it. These are the classic pitfalls you need to be aware of. If you dodge these traps and stay sharp, your sales process will run smoother than a well-oiled machine, and you'll see results that keep you smiling all the way to the bank.

Final Thoughts

if you take anything away from this chapter, let it be this: **Sales is a process, not a game of chance.** It's not about hitting people over the head with your product and hoping they'll buy. It's about creating a system, understanding your customer's needs, and then offering the right solution at the right time. Just like that Army recruiter who saw through my BS and found a way to match my energy and needs, your sales process needs to do the same. **Listen, adapt, and know when to ask for the sale.**

You can have the best product in the world, but if your sales process isn't dialed in, it's like driving a Ferrari with no engine. You've got to ask the right questions, follow up like a persistent pitbull, and close deals with confidence. Don't let the chaos of chasing deals take over—build a solid system, track your results, and refine your approach.

If you take the time to implement a solid sales process and avoid these common pitfalls, your business won't just grow—it'll thrive. You'll go from guessing where your next sale is coming from to knowing exactly where to aim. So get out there, build your sales process, and start closing like the pro you're meant to be.

No more cold calls in the dark. It's time to hunt with purpose, not just hope.

Let's Put This Into Action

"Help me create a step-by-step sales process for my business. I want the process to be systematic and repeatable, yet flexible enough to adapt to the needs of different customers. The process should include the following stages: initial lead qualification, how to approach the prospect, presenting the product/service, handling objections, and closing the sale. Please also help me identify key actions and questions for each stage, and suggest ways to track and measure success. I want this sales process to help me close more deals and build stronger relationships with my customers."

☆ ⭐ ☆

Chapter 10:
LEADERSHIP

Let me tell you about my first day at Fort Campbell, part of the 101st Airborne Division. I was a fresh E2, just out of basic, wide-eyed and trying to figure out where the hell I was going. It was my first real taste of military life outside of training. And that day, my company commander told me I had to report to PT with the brigade commander. Now, as an E2, I had never even spoken to a full-bird colonel before, let alone run alongside one. So, I'm thinking, "Okay, this will be interesting."

I didn't think much of it at first—after all, I was in great shape. Always had been. I was the guy who crushed every run back at basic, barely breaking a sweat while others were gasping for air. So, no big deal. Just another PT session, right?

Well, turns out, that "no big deal" PT session ended up being my first glimpse of what excellent leadership looks like.

We start the run, and the brigade commander is setting a solid pace. We stop a few miles in, and at first, I think, "Okay, maybe he's getting tired. It's been a few miles." But no, this guy's not winded at all—he stops near a street sign, looks up, and points.

"See that street sign? That's named after a battle our unit fought in WWII. Let me tell you what went down there."

He wasn't just giving us some history lesson. He was telling us about the soldiers who fought, the challenges they faced, and the real price of what we were about to be a part of. His words weren't just facts; they were stories. And the way he told them, it hit you. You could almost hear the footsteps of those soldiers beside you, the weight of their history in every word.

By the time that run was over, I wasn't just pumped about getting through the PT session. I felt like I was connected to a legacy. I was stepping into a unit with a history of excellence, and that brigade commander was making sure we understood it from the very beginning.

A few months later, we're gearing up to head to Afghanistan. That same brigade commander steps up before we board the plane and gives us one last speech. And let me tell you, this guy doesn't sugarcoat anything. He straight-up tells us we're about to face some of the toughest challenges of our lives. He tells us vivid stories of the unit that came before us—their struggles, the battles they fought, the sacrifices they made. He paints the picture of the tough days we're going to face: long days in the heat, unpredictable enemies, and moments when we'll be pushed to our absolute limits.

But then, he pivots and says, "But when we roll in, we're not backing down. We're going to match evil with fierce offensive aggression. We are the unit that will make the difference."

"You've trained for this. You are the best damn fighting force the world has ever seen, and you are ready to show it."

By the time we boarded that plane, we weren't just a group of soldiers; we were a brotherhood, fired up and ready to take on the world. Every single one of us knew we were there for a purpose and were ready to make an impact.

Now, here's the thing: throughout the deployment, it wasn't just the speeches. It was how he led. This commander wasn't just a guy with a mic making speeches while we did all the heavy lifting. No, he was always the first one on the ground, always in the thick of the action, and always the last one to leave. He set the example every single time. And the results spoke for themselves.

We were part of some of the biggest operations of the entire war, and it was all because of leadership like that. Leadership that wasn't just talk—it was in every action, every decision, and every time he showed up when things were tough. He made us feel like we were doing something bigger than ourselves. That we were part of something with purpose, with meaning, and damn if it didn't make a difference.

So, what does this story have to do with business? Everything.

Leadership is the final ingredient in your business's growth. You can have the best product, the best marketing, the best systems, but without leadership, none of it matters. It's leadership that takes those individual parts and makes them work together to form something greater. It's leadership that inspires your team to give their best, that creates a culture of excellence, and that helps everyone understand the mission, no matter how tough things get.

It's the kind of leadership that makes people feel like they're part of something big—something worth investing in. And just like that brigade commander, you don't just lead by telling people what to do. You lead by showing up, by setting the example, and by making every person on your team feel like they are vital to the mission.

In business, that kind of leadership isn't optional. It's the key to taking your team from ordinary to extraordinary. And that, my friend, is how you build something that lasts.

So, What Makes a Great Leader?

Here's the thing about leadership—it's not about having a title or barking orders from your fancy corner office. Anyone can do that. Leadership's about influence. It's about having the guts to take responsibility for everything, good or bad, and being willing to drag your team through the tough stuff when they don't feel like it. It's about being the one who stays cool when everyone else loses their heads. A great leader isn't just someone in charge—they're the ones that get their people to believe in the vision, make them feel like part of the mission, and get their asses moving when it matters.

Now, responsibility? That's the bedrock of leadership. If your team fails, guess what? That's on you. If they succeed, you get to take credit, but deep down, you know who the real MVP is. That's the price you pay for leadership, and it's not for the faint of heart. You'll get all the blame and most of the stress, but you'll also get the most rewarding feeling when things go right.

Great leaders don't shy away from making the tough calls. They don't kick the can down the road hoping someone else will handle it. They step up, face the fire, and make decisions that could make or break the business. They get that leadership isn't just about being the boss—it's about having the guts to make decisions, even when the odds are stacked against you. And they don't do it alone—they're pulling the team in with them every step of the way.

Empathy? Yeah, you heard me right. Leadership isn't just about strategy and structure; it's about understanding your people. You think all your employees are robots who show up, work, and then go home? Wake up. Every single one of them has a different story. They have different strengths, weaknesses, fears, and motivations. A leader knows this and listens. It's about recognizing that your team isn't a machine—it's a living, breathing group of people, and if you can't lead them with empathy, you're screwed. No one is going to follow a cold, heartless robot. They follow someone who gets them and supports them through the grind.

But here's the kicker—without trust, you've got nothing. Trust is the glue that holds it all together. It's what makes the difference between a team that falls apart when things get tough and a team that keeps pushing through. Build trust by being honest, even when the truth is uncomfortable. Be consistent. Don't flip-flop. Your people need to know you'll stand by them, and when they trust you, they'll follow you through hell and back.

Now, a great leader doesn't just have a vision—they can communicate that vision in a way that gets everyone on board. If you can't paint a clear picture of what success looks like, then you've got a problem. Your team needs to understand why they're doing what they're doing and how their piece of the puzzle fits into the larger mission. If they don't get that, you're going to have a bunch of people doing busy work without any real direction.

Lastly, the best leaders are always learning. They don't stop growing just because they've climbed a few rungs on the ladder. If you think you've got it all figured out, you're already behind. The most successful leaders are the ones who know they don't have all the answers and are constantly improving, whether it's through reading, taking courses, or just listening to their team. A great leader is always looking for ways to be better, not just for themselves but for their team and the business as a whole.

So, here's the deal—being a great leader isn't about sitting in an office with a title and a corner view. It's about being in the trenches with your people, knowing when to step up and take responsibility, making the tough calls, building trust, communicating clearly, and always improving. When you've got that mindset, you'll build more than just a business—you'll build a legacy of leadership.

How to Create a Leadership Strategy

Now that we've talked about what makes a great leader, let's get down to the real work: building a leadership strategy for your organization. Because here's the truth—if you don't have a plan for leadership, then you're flying by the seat of your pants, hoping you can figure it out as you go. And let me tell you, that's a quick way to lose your team and stall your growth.

A leadership strategy isn't just a nice-to-have; it's the blueprint for how your entire organization is going to operate, grow, and hit its targets. It's about creating a system where your leadership isn't just a few strong voices at the top, but a network of leaders throughout your business who are driving results, inspiring action, and making sure your people are working toward a common goal.

The first thing to understand when creating your leadership strategy is that it starts with yourself. That's right. You, the leader, are the foundation of the whole thing. You can't lead your team to excellence if you're not leading by example. If you're not walking the walk, no one else will follow. The strategy begins with you, so take a long look at your own leadership style and make sure you're setting the standard you want everyone else to follow.

But that's just the beginning. Once you've got yourself dialed in, you need to identify the future leaders in your organization. Not everyone is going to step up on their own, and that's okay. It's your job to spot potential and start developing your next generation of leaders. This means looking beyond just the top performers—great leaders don't always come from the people who are the loudest or the ones who have the most experience. A strong leader is someone who owns the mission, empowers their team, and takes responsibility—and you need to build your leadership pipeline with people who show these traits.

Next, let's talk about delegating leadership roles and setting clear expectations. A strong leadership strategy doesn't mean you're doing everything yourself or micromanaging every single thing that happens. It's about setting clear roles, responsibilities, and giving your leaders the space to take ownership. Each leader within your organization should have a specific area to lead, whether it's operations, sales, marketing, or customer service. They need the autonomy to make decisions, but they also need the accountability to make sure their actions align with your overall mission.

Finally, a great leadership strategy includes ongoing development. You don't just set your leaders up and leave them to figure it out. Leadership is a continuous growth process. You need to provide your team with the resources, the training, and the feedback they need to grow into the best versions of themselves. Set up regular check-ins, workshops, and opportunities for your leaders to learn from each other. Leadership doesn't just happen in a vacuum—it thrives in a culture of constant feedback and evolution.

So, here's the deal—building a leadership strategy is about much more than just having a few strong people at the top. It's about creating a leadership culture that flows throughout your organization, where everyone is empowered, held accountable, and aligned with your mission. It's about developing the right people, setting clear roles, and constantly refining the process. Leadership isn't a one-time event. It's an ongoing strategy that has to be nurtured and built from the ground up. If you do it right, it won't just be your company that grows—it'll be your team too.

Common Pitfalls To Avoid

1. Thinking Leadership is All About You

Listen, I get it. You started the company. You've probably worked harder than anyone to get where you are, and it's easy to think that your leadership is what's going to carry the whole damn thing. News flash: you're not Superman. Leadership is **not** about you standing at the front and barking orders all day long. If you want your team to follow you, you've got to be willing to **develop other leaders**—and that doesn't happen if you're constantly trying to do everything yourself. If you're not actively building your leadership pipeline, your company will get stuck because everyone will be waiting for **you** to make every decision. You need to step back and let other leaders rise up. It's about empowering them, not micromanaging them.

2. Failing to Communicate the Vision

Here's the deal: You might have the greatest vision for your business in your head, but if you don't **communicate** that vision to your team, it's as useful as a tank with no fuel. If your leaders don't know what the hell they're working toward, they're just going through the motions. So, don't assume that your vision is self-explanatory. You've got to talk about it—often. **Paint the picture** for your team so they understand the "why" behind the work they're doing. Great leadership isn't just about giving orders. It's about inspiring your team to push themselves because they know why it matters.

3. Ignoring Accountability

There's nothing worse than having a bunch of leaders who are technically in charge of something, but no one's holding them accountable for their results. Leadership isn't a free pass to coast. If you're not holding your leaders accountable, then they're probably not doing their job as well as they should. And the worst part is, the rest of your team notices. If there's no accountability, your team gets complacent, and your culture goes to crap. Holding people accountable is uncomfortable, but it's **absolutely necessary**. If your leaders are floundering or making excuses, don't sweep it under the rug—call them out and get them back on track.

4. Not Investing in Development

So, you've got some leaders on your team—great. But here's the thing: leaders are **never done** learning. You can't just give them a title and expect them to be perfect. Leadership is an **ongoing** process, and if you're not investing in your leaders' development, then you're leaving money on the table. Whether it's through training, mentorship, or hands-on experience, your leaders need **constant growth**. If you don't provide that for them, don't be surprised when they hit a wall or, worse, leave the company to find it somewhere else. Leadership development isn't a one-time thing; it's a lifelong commitment.

5. Letting Ego Get in the Way

Here's the biggest pitfall that I've seen take down so many leaders: letting their **ego** run the show. If you're letting your pride get in the way of doing what's best for your team and your company, you're in trouble. Ego can be a killer when it comes to leadership. It makes you defensive. It blinds you to feedback. And it makes you refuse to listen when people challenge your decisions. A good leader isn't too proud to admit when they're wrong or when they need help. If your ego is running the show, you're not leading—you're just throwing a tantrum. Get over it. **Great leaders are humble** and open to feedback—whether it's from their team or from a tough situation.

6. Underestimating the Importance of Culture

You can have all the best systems and processes in place, but if your culture sucks, it's all for nothing. The culture of your organization is like the foundation of a building. If it's shaky, everything else is at risk of crumbling. You can have all the right people, the right processes, and the right goals—but if your culture doesn't promote **trust, collaboration, and respect**, you'll never get the results you want. Great leadership shapes culture. It's a daily practice. It's about setting the tone for how people treat each other, how they show up to work, and how they work together to solve problems. If you don't have that figured out, your team is going to fall apart quicker than you can say "leadership failure."

7. Not Giving People a Chance to Lead

This one's simple: if you're not giving your people the **opportunity** to lead, then you're not developing them. You're keeping them in the dark, and that's doing them—and your business—a disservice. Leadership development isn't about just telling people what to do. It's about giving them the chance to step up, make decisions, and take responsibility. If you're constantly in "do it for them" mode, your team is never going to grow, and neither will your business.

So, don't make these mistakes. A strong leadership strategy doesn't come together overnight—it's a constant, evolving process. You'll hit bumps along the way, but if you stay humble, keep the lines of communication open, hold your team accountable, and invest in leadership development, you'll build a team that's not only effective but unstoppable.

Final Thoughts

Leadership isn't just about sitting at the top and telling everyone what to do. It's about **guiding, motivating, and developing** others to take ownership and step up. The best leaders don't just manage—they **create more leaders.** They lay the groundwork, set the pace, and empower others to rise to the occasion.

A successful leadership strategy is built on the principles of responsibility, accountability, empathy, trust, and the ability to communicate a compelling vision. As a leader, it's your job to give your team the tools, the resources, and the confidence they need to succeed. But it's also your job to step back when needed, make tough decisions when required, and continue learning to stay at the top of your game.

Now, it's time for you to step up and put all this into action. Don't just sit around hoping for results—**lead**. Build your leadership strategy, develop your people, and watch how your business transforms. A great team doesn't happen by accident. It happens because you, as a leader, create an environment where people thrive, grow, and give their best. Now, go out there and show them how it's done.

Great leadership isn't just the cherry on top of a business—it's the engine that makes everything run. It's what turns a group of people into a high-performing team, and a business from surviving to thriving. So, roll up your sleeves, get to work, and be the leader you were meant to be.

Let's Put This Into Action

"Help me create a leadership strategy for my organization. I want to develop a plan that will inspire, empower, and develop my team to reach their full potential. The strategy should focus on the key leadership attributes such as responsibility, empathy, trust-building, and effective communication. Please help me identify the leadership structure, the key behaviors to model, and the specific actions I need to take to guide my team toward success. Additionally, suggest ways to align my leadership style with the company's goals, and provide strategies for fostering a culture of leadership at all levels of the organization."

GOLD PHASE: SCALING AND SUSTAINING

Chapter 11:
SCALING

When I first started coaching, I had a client—let's call him Jake—who was stuck in what's known as the classic founder's dilemma. On the surface, everything looked golden. Jake's businesses were thriving on paper: profits were up, employees were busy, and clients were happy. But behind the scenes, the guy was barely holding it together. He wasn't lazy—far from it. He was one of the hardest-working, most driven people I'd ever met. But that drive had become a double-edged sword.

Jake's day-to-day life was a nightmare. His phone might as well have been surgically attached to his hand. Calls, texts, emails—it never stopped. If one of his managers sneezed, Jake knew about it before they reached for a tissue. Every minor decision, every small issue, it all funneled directly to him. Jake was the bottleneck in his businesses, the hub that everything revolved around. And because of that, nothing moved unless he was actively involved.

Then Jake landed the contract of a lifetime—the kind of deal that most entrepreneurs dream about. It should've been a victory lap, a moment of celebration. Instead, it turned into his worst nightmare. The new contract meant more work, more decisions, and more fires to put out. Jake wasn't just overwhelmed—he was completely underwater. What should've been his proudest moment was quickly becoming his breaking point.

When we sat down to talk, the problem was clear. Jake's businesses weren't running like a system—they were running like a hamster wheel, powered entirely by him. If Jake stopped running, the whole thing would collapse. It wasn't just unsustainable—it was dangerous.

The first thing we did was a deep dive into his businesses. We mapped out everything he was doing himself—from approving invoices to responding to customer complaints. Then, we built an ideal organizational chart. Not one based on what Jake currently had, but one based on what his businesses needed to run smoothly without him micromanaging every step.

The next step was empowering his team. Jake had smart, capable managers, but he hadn't given them the authority to make decisions. Every choice, no matter how small, landed on his desk. We created clear roles and responsibilities, assigning tasks to the managers and giving them ownership over their areas. It wasn't easy for Jake to let go—founders are notoriously bad at delegation—but as his team stepped up, he began to see the difference.

His managers weren't just keeping the wheels turning—they were driving the businesses forward. They spotted inefficiencies, identified new opportunities, and started making decisions that Jake didn't have to second-guess. For the first time, Jake wasn't managing chaos; he was leading a team.

But there was still one piece missing: technology.

We introduced automation tools to handle the repetitive, time-consuming tasks that were eating up his team's time. A CRM system was implemented to manage customer interactions and automate follow-ups. Project management software kept his teams organized and ensured deadlines were met. Jake even started using AI tools for customer service, which cut response times in half and freed up his employees to focus on higher-value tasks.

The impact was immediate. Tasks that used to take hours were now being handled in minutes. Jake's team wasn't bogged down with busywork anymore—they were free to focus on growth. And because these systems didn't require more manpower, Jake's overhead stayed the same while his efficiency skyrocketed.

As Jake's businesses became more streamlined, something unexpected happened. The new contract that had once overwhelmed him became the catalyst for exponential growth. His companies weren't just surviving—they were thriving. Each business began feeding into the others, creating a synergy that amplified their success. One company would land a deal, and the others would provide complementary services, creating a ripple effect that boosted revenue across the board.

Jake went from being a stressed-out bottleneck to a confident leader. He wasn't putting out fires anymore—he was building an empire. The businesses were running smoothly, the flywheel was spinning, and for the first time in years, Jake had time to focus on the bigger picture.

Here's the takeaway: Scaling isn't about working harder. It's about working smarter. It's about empowering your team, leveraging technology, and creating systems that allow your business to grow without you holding it together with duct tape. Scaling is about freedom—not just for your business, but for you. And when you get it right, the results speak for themselves.

So, what makes good scaling?

Let's clear something up right out of the gate: growth and scaling aren't the same thing. People love to throw these words around like they're interchangeable, but they're not. Growth is when your business gets bigger because you're pouring more resources into it— more time, more money, more people. Scaling, on the other hand, is when your business gets bigger without a proportional increase in resources. It's like going from pushing a boulder uphill to rolling it downhill. Same boulder, but a hell of a lot less effort.

Here's the harsh truth: most business owners are stuck in growth mode, thinking they're scaling when really they're just working harder. They keep adding more customers, more employees, and more hours to their workweek, but their profit margins stay the same—or worse, they shrink. If you're constantly hiring more people to keep up with demand or spending more money just to maintain the status quo, guess what? You're growing, but you're not scaling. And that's a dangerous place to be.

Scaling is a whole different beast. It's about leveraging systems, people, and technology to create a business that can handle more work, more clients, and more revenue without you burning out or breaking the bank. It's about creating momentum so that your business grows exponentially, not linearly.

Now, let's talk about what makes good scaling. Good scaling has a few key components, and if you get these right, you'll be well on your way to building a business that can grow without you having to push every step of the way. Let's break it down.

First, scaling requires the right leadership structure. You can't scale if every decision has to go through you. If you're still approving every invoice, answering every email, and solving every problem, you're not scaling—you're micromanaging. Businesses that scale have leaders, not just employees waiting to be told what to do. You need people in key roles who can think critically, solve problems, and take ownership of their responsibilities without needing your constant input. This means identifying the right people in your organization and empowering them to step up. And no, empowerment doesn't just mean saying "I trust you" and walking away. It means setting clear expectations, giving them the tools they need, and letting them know they have your support. It also means getting out of their way. If you're hovering over every decision, you're not empowering anyone—you're just creating another bottleneck.

Next, scaling hinges on processes that let your business grow without buckling under the weight. If you're building a house, you don't start with the roof—you lay a foundation that can support the whole structure. The same goes for your business. Scaling demands systems designed to handle more—more clients, more orders, more complexity—without you holding it all together. Think of client onboarding: when you go from ten customers to a hundred, a handshake and a quick chat won't cut it—you need a documented workflow that tracks every step, from first contact to follow-up, so nothing slips. Or take order fulfillment: as volume spikes, a checklist or automated tracking system keeps deliveries on time without you chasing every package. These aren't just any Standard Operating Procedures (SOPs)—they're the playbooks that turn growth into a machine, not a mess. They let your team execute flawlessly at scale, freeing you to lead instead of micromanage. The goal? A business that thrives under pressure, not one that crashes mid-flight.

Third, you need a financial plan. Let me be blunt: you can grow yourself right into bankruptcy if you're not careful. Scaling costs money, and if you're not managing your finances wisely, you're going to run out of cash. This is one of the biggest mistakes business owners make when trying to scale. They get excited about growth and start throwing money at new hires, new products, and new marketing campaigns without a clear plan for how to pay for it all. Good scaling means managing your cash flow and aligning your growth with your revenue goals. You need to know when to reinvest, when to raise capital, and when to pull back and regroup. It's not about being cheap—it's about being smart with your resources. Understand your profit margins, track your cash flow, and keep an eye on your burn rate. Scaling isn't just about making more money—it's about keeping more of what you make. If you're not profitable, you're not scaling. You're sinking.

Finally, let's talk about technology. This is the game-changer that allows you to scale without adding more people or increasing costs. Technology lets you do more with less. You've already seen how automation tools, project management software, and AI can take tasks off your plate and streamline your operations. But the key to using technology effectively is to focus on automation and integration. Don't just throw tools at problems—use tools that actually solve problems. For example, a Customer Relationship Management (CRM) system can automate your follow-ups, track your leads, and manage your customer interactions without you having to lift a finger. Project management tools can keep your team organized and ensure deadlines are met. And AI-powered chatbots can handle customer service inquiries, saving your team hours of work each week. The goal of using technology isn't just to make things faster—it's to make things easier. It reduces your dependency on manual labor and allows your business to handle more work without increasing headcount.

Scaling means growing without breaking—building a machine that runs efficiently, not one you have to push uphill every day. It's about having the right people, the right systems, a solid financial plan, and the right technology to keep things moving forward. When you've got those pieces in place, scaling becomes a lot less scary. It's not about grinding harder or adding more hours to your day. It's about setting up a machine that can run efficiently and grow without you having to push every step of the way. Scaling is how you go from working in your business to working on your business.

And here's the best part: once you start scaling, the momentum builds itself. Your business becomes a flywheel that keeps turning, even when you're not there to push it. That's the magic of scaling. It's not about hustling harder. It's about building smarter. So the real question is—are you ready to scale, or are you still stuck managing chaos?

How to start scaling your business?

Now that you understand what makes good scaling, it's time to talk about how to actually make it happen in your business. Let's be real— knowing what scaling looks like is one thing. Creating it is a whole different animal.

Maybe you're thinking, *That all sounds great, but where the hell do I even start?* You're not alone. Most business owners get stuck right there, staring at their chaotic day-to-day operations and wondering how to turn that mess into a well-oiled machine.

Here's the good news: if you've been following this book so far, you're already halfway there. You've got your vision, your mission, your strategy. You've started building systems, defining roles, and delegating tasks. You're already laying the foundation for scaling, whether you realize it or not.

The first step to scaling your business is getting yourself out of the weeds. If you're the person who's answering every question, solving every problem, and approving every decision, you're not running a scalable business—you're running a glorified circus, and you're the ringmaster. Scaling starts with building a leadership structure that can stand on its own without you constantly pulling the strings. You need people who are capable, trusted, and empowered to take ownership of their roles.

Start by asking yourself this: If I took a month off, would my business survive? If the answer is no, you've got work to do. The first thing you need is an organizational chart that shows how your business is structured—not just what it looks like now, but what it needs to look like for your business to scale. What roles are missing? What tasks are you still doing that should be someone else's responsibility? Write it down. Map it out. The goal is to replace yourself in as many day-to-day functions as possible.

Now, this doesn't mean you disappear and let the whole thing run on autopilot. It means setting your team up for success by giving them clear roles, responsibilities, and the authority to make decisions without coming to you for approval every five minutes. If you've already got people in leadership roles, ask yourself: Are they actually leading, or are they waiting for me to tell them what to do? If it's the latter, it's time to change that.

Once your leadership structure is in place, the next step is to focus on systems and processes. Scaling isn't about making your business bigger; it's about making it more efficient. That means taking a hard look at your current operations and identifying where the bottlenecks are. Where are things getting stuck? Where are mistakes happening? Where are you losing time or money? These are the areas where you need systems in place.

Start with the tasks that happen most often—the repetitive, predictable things that eat up time. If you're constantly answering the same questions from customers, create an FAQ or set up an automated chatbot to handle those inquiries. If your team is spending hours tracking invoices, implement a system that automates billing and payments. The goal is to streamline your operations so that things happen consistently and predictably, without needing you to step in and micromanage every process.

But let's be clear: systems don't have to be complicated. Some of the best systems are simple checklists and workflows that ensure nothing falls through the cracks. The key is to document everything. If there's a process that happens more than once, write it down. Create a playbook that your team can follow so that you're not the only person who knows how things are supposed to get done.

Once you've got your systems in place, it's time to focus on financial alignment. One of the biggest mistakes business owners make when trying to scale is overextending themselves financially. They assume that scaling means spending more money—hiring more people, buying more equipment, launching more products—but that's how businesses end up growing broke. Scaling isn't about throwing money at growth; it's about using your resources wisely and aligning your revenue goals with your growth strategy.

This is where cash flow management becomes critical. You need to know where your money is coming from, where it's going, and how much runway you have before you need to raise capital or pull back on spending. Set clear revenue targets for each stage of your growth, and make sure your spending aligns with those targets. If you're not keeping an eye on your numbers, scaling can quickly turn into a disaster.

Finally, let's talk about technology. If you want to scale without adding more people or increasing your costs, technology is your best friend. But here's the key: don't use technology for the sake of it. Use it to solve real problems and make your life easier.

Start by looking at where your team is spending the most time. Are they spending hours manually following up with clients? Implement a CRM system to automate follow-ups and track leads. Are they constantly juggling deadlines and tasks? Use project management tools to keep everything on track. Are you still doing payroll manually? Automate that too. The point isn't to replace your team with robots (unless you're running a robot business), but to free up their time so they can focus on high-value work that actually moves the business forward.

One of my clients implemented a simple AI-driven customer service tool that handled basic inquiries and routed more complex issues to the right team member. It saved his team hours of work each week and improved response times for customers. Another client used automated workflows to handle routine admin tasks like scheduling and invoicing, which meant his team could focus on bigger-picture projects instead of getting bogged down in busy work. Technology isn't a magic bullet, but when used correctly, it's a game-changer for scaling efficiently.

So, let's sum it up. Creating scaling in your business comes down to four things: leadership, systems, financial alignment, and technology. You need the right people in the right roles, clear processes that keep things running smoothly, a financial plan that keeps you on track, and tools that help you do more with less. It's not about working harder—it's about building a machine that can run without you.

Scaling isn't something that happens overnight. It's a process. But if you take it step by step, your business will start to grow beyond you. The flywheel will start spinning, and you'll go from managing chaos to leading growth.

The only question left is: Are you ready to step back from the day-to-day and start building something that lasts?

Scaling Checklist for Your Team

Scaling your business in the Blue Phase means growing your team's impact without chaos. Use this checklist to guide your squad:

- **Assess Capacity**: Can your current team handle 20% more orders? Measure output—e.g., a bakery's 5-person crew baked 200 loaves weekly; scaling to 240 needs process tweaks.

- **Strengthen Systems**: Update SOPs for new volume—e.g., automate inventory tracking if sales rise 30%.

- **Train Your Crew**: Invest 5 hours weekly in team training—e.g., a retail team learned new POS software, cutting checkout time by 15%.

- **Test Demand**: Pilot a 10% sales increase for 30 days—track if customer satisfaction dips below 90%.

- **Secure Cash Flow**: Ensure 3 months' expenses in reserve—e.g., a service business with 7 employees saved $15,000 to cover scaling costs.

Scaling is a make-or-break moment: 50% of small businesses fail after growing without solid systems. This checklist for your squad—

covering team roles, cash flow, and processes—guards against that pitfall.

Case Study: A cleaning company with an 8-person team scaled from 10 to 15 clients weekly. They assessed capacity (team handled 12 easily), strengthened systems with a scheduling app, trained staff on new routes, tested with 13 clients (satisfaction stayed at 95%), and secured $20,000 in reserves. Result? A 40% revenue jump in four months without burnout. Their success hinged on clear roles—studies show teams with defined responsibilities grow 30% faster. Use this to align your crew and sustain that growth momentum.

Use this checklist to scale your team's efforts, illuminating your path forward.

Common Pitfalls To Avoid

1. Trying to Do Everything at Once

This is probably the most common mistake I see. A business owner gets excited about growth and suddenly wants to launch five new products, open two new locations, and hire a dozen people—all at the same time. Guess what happens? Chaos. The business ends up spread too thin, and everything suffers

2. Failing to Trust Your Team

Let me be blunt: if you can't trust your team, you're screwed. I've worked with business owners who couldn't delegate because they were convinced no one could do things as well as they could. You know where those businesses are now? Nowhere. If you're stuck micromanaging every detail, you're never going to scale. You've got to empower your team to make decisions and trust them to handle their responsibilities. And yes, mistakes will happen. But guess what? That's how people learn.

3. Ignoring Cash Flow

I've said it before, and I'll say it again: you can grow yourself broke. One of the most dangerous pitfalls in scaling is overextending your finances. Business owners get caught up in growth mode, spending money on new hires, new tools, and new projects, without keeping a close eye on cash flow. Next thing you know, the bills are piling up, and the cash isn't coming in fast enough to cover them.

4. Adding People Before Adding Systems

Here's a trap that a lot of business owners fall into: they assume that scaling means hiring more people. They hit a growth spurt, and the first thing they do is throw bodies at the problem—hire more sales reps, more customer service staff, more project managers. But here's the thing: if you don't have systems in place, more people just means more chaos.

5. Forgetting About Culture

When businesses start to scale, culture often takes a backseat. The focus shifts to revenue, growth, and operations, and the human side of the business gets neglected. But here's the thing: your culture is what holds everything together. It's what keeps your team motivated, engaged, and aligned with your vision.

6. Thinking Technology Will Fix Everything

We've talked about the importance of technology in scaling, but let me be clear: technology isn't a magic bullet. I've seen business owners blow thousands of dollars on fancy tools and software that they never actually use. Why? Because they thought tech would fix their problems without addressing the underlying issues.

7. Thinking Scaling Means Stepping Away Completely

Here's one I've seen too many times: a business owner thinks that scaling means they can finally step away and let the business run itself. They picture themselves on a beach somewhere, sipping cocktails while their team handles everything. Let me break it to you: that's not how this works. Scaling doesn't mean you disappear. It means you shift your focus. Instead of managing day-to-day operations, you're leading the business, setting the vision, and driving growth. You're still very much involved—you're just in a different role.

Final Thoughts

Scaling isn't about doing more work—it's about building smarter systems and trusting your team to run them. It's about shifting from being the business's bottleneck to leading its growth. If you're still at the center of every decision, you're not scaling—you're just treading water.

By now, you've laid the groundwork. You've clarified your vision, defined your mission, and built systems to keep the day-to-day chaos in check. The next step is to step back. Let your systems and your people take the reins, while you focus on leading the business to new opportunities.

Scaling won't happen overnight, and it won't happen without intention. But if you stay focused on empowering your team, aligning your finances, and leveraging technology, you'll see the momentum build. The flywheel will start spinning, and the business will grow—without you having to push every piece along.

So, ask yourself: What's holding you back from scaling? Identify it, fix it, and get out of your own way. It's time to build something that runs smoothly and grows without breaking you in the process.

☆★☆

Chapter 12:

INNOVATION

A pizza shop owner I coached—let's call him Tony—was famous for hand-tossed, wood-fired pizzas, but success brought chaos for his small team of five. Customers poured in, the phone rang off the hook, and Tony's crew was maxed out. His kitchen had no space for more hands, and labor costs teetered on the edge. As a small team leader in the Blue Phase of FOGS, Tony needed to grow without breaking his squad. That's when he turned to a skill I learned in the military: Field-Expedient Innovation—the art of solving problems with what's at hand, no matter the constraints.

Tony rallied his team like a soldier:

- **Assess**: He took stock with his crew—tight budget, small kitchen, but a loyal customer base. Together, they pinpointed the core issues: dough prep ate hours, and ordering chaos caused errors during peak times.

- **Adapt**: He directed his team to repurpose what they had. For dough, he invested in a semi-automatic dough press—a one-time cost that cut prep time in half, freeing his staff to focus elsewhere while maintaining consistency. For orders, he tasked a tech-savvy employee to launch an online system, letting customers pick toppings, set times, and prepay—all without adding staff.

- **Act**: Tony tested the dough press with his team for a week—it worked, boosting morale as they saw results. The online system rolled out next, with his crew refining it based on feedback, slashing errors and boosting efficiency. Within months, online orders hit 60% of sales, customer satisfaction soared, and his team—now less overwhelmed—brainstormed new specials that drove even more growth.

Tony didn't need a bigger kitchen or more staff. He turned constraints into catalysts, using Field-Expedient Innovation to lead his squad to unlock Growth without breaking.

What Is Field-Expedient Innovation?

Innovation isn't about flashy ideas or endless budgets—it's a mindset: finding smarter, better, or different ways to get the job done. In the military, we call this Field-Expedient Innovation: adapting in the field when resources are scarce and stakes are high. It's not about inventing something new—it's about making what you have work better, like jury-rigging a tool to survive a mission. In business, it's the same: streamlining a process, adopting a tool, or rethinking your approach to save time, cut costs, or boost results.

You don't need to be Steve Jobs unveiling the iPhone. Sometimes, it's as simple as asking, "How can I make this less of a headache?" But it takes guts. You'll need to admit something's not working, ditch the "we've always done it this way" trap, and take a risk on the untested. It's messy, uncomfortable, and humbling—but the payoff is worth it. Whether it's shaving hours off your week, doubling your revenue, or just sleeping better at night, innovation moves you from stuck to unstoppable in the Blue Phase of FOGS.

How to Innovate Like a Soldier: Assess, Adapt, Act

Soldiers don't innovate with endless resources—they do it with what's in their pack, under fire. I'll never forget a mission in Afghanistan when our convoy's GPS failed. We couldn't communicate with the other trucks or our higher headquarters, and we had no spares. One of my soldiers assessed our gear—we had a paper map and a compass buried in a pack. He adapted by rigging the compass to the map with duct tape, marking our route by hand. We acted, moving cautiously, checking landmarks, and adjusting as we went. That field-expedient solution got us to base safely.

That's Field-Expedient Innovation, and it boils down to three steps you can use to spark Growth with your team:

- **Assess:** Take stock with your crew—your resources, constraints, and the problem. In the field, this means checking gear and terrain with your squad; in business, it's your budget, team skills, and customer needs. Ask: What's the core issue, and what can my team leverage?

- **Adapt:** Direct your team to repurpose what's at hand. Soldiers might repurpose a tool—like using a tent pole as a splint; you might guide your crew to repurpose a process, like using an existing email list to test a new offer. Creativity within limits is the key.

- **Act:** Lead your team to test the solution fast, learn from the results, and adjust. In combat, you don't wait for perfect—you act and adapt on the fly. In business, launch small with your squad, measure the impact, and refine based on their input.

Tony's story shows this in action—he assessed his limits, adapted with tools he could afford, and acted to test and refine. That's how you innovate without breaking.

Common Pitfalls to Avoid

Field-Expedient Innovation is powerful, but it's not foolproof. Here are the traps that can derail your efforts—and how to sidestep them:

Overcomplicating: Don't add unnecessary complexity. Focus on solving the problem, not showing off.

Stalling Out: Overthinking kills momentum. Act fast—test small, refine later.

Ignoring Your Team: Changes fail without buy-in. Involve your team early and explain the why.

Chasing Fads: Don't jump on trends that don't fit your goals. Innovate with purpose.

Giving Up Early: First tries might stumble. Treat setbacks as feedback, not failure.

Skipping Metrics: You can't improve what you don't measure. Track results to know what works.

Forgetting Customers: If it doesn't serve your customers, it's a distraction. Always ask: How does this help them?

Dodge these pitfalls by staying focused and practical. Innovation isn't about perfection—it's about progress.

Innovation in Action: Your Turn

Innovation upgrades your playbook, turning good processes into great ones that fuel Growth for your team in the Blue Phase of FOGS. Tony didn't need a second location—he needed a soldier's mindset to lead his squad with what he had. Now it's your turn, small team leader. Where is your crew stuck? What process is draining your team's time or your budget? What's the one change you can direct your squad to spark momentum?

Field-Expedient Innovation isn't a one-off—it's a habit. Keep assessing, adapting, and acting, and you'll turn every challenge into an opportunity. As you march toward Sustainability, this mindset will keep your business sharp, resilient, and ready for whatever the battlefield throws next. So, start small, start now—because the only thing worse than failing at innovation is staying stuck and never trying.

Let's Put This Into Action

A.I. Prompt: Use AI to kickstart your Field-Expedient Innovation. Prompt ChatGPT with: *'I'm a [your business type] with limited resources—budget of [your budget], team of [your team size]. What innovative solution can I create to [specific problem] using only what I have?'* Use the results to assess your resources, adapt a solution, and plan your next action."

Bonus

Need ideas to start innovating today? I've compiled my top 5 field-expedient strategies small businesses use to make a big impact without breaking the bank. These are practical, battle-tested solutions you can deploy now. Head to my website to download them for free https://tgscoaching.com/resources/. Too much effort to type? Scan the QR code below.

☆✰☆

Chapter 13:
OVERCOMING OBSTACLES

Let me tell you about something we runners call "the bonk." It's not just a term—it's a rite of passage. The bonk is that moment in a marathon when your body, your mind, and even your spirit seems to betray you. For me, it's as predictable as sunrise. No matter how much I train, no matter how prepared I feel, the bonk always shows up. And it doesn't come quietly. It barges in like an unwelcome guest, throwing everything into chaos.

It starts small. A hot spot on my foot feels like someone lit a match. My shorts rubbing against my lower back? Suddenly, it's a belt of sandpaper. Every breath feels heavier, every step harder. And then come the voices. "Why are you doing this? You don't have to prove anything to anyone. Just stop. Nobody's watching, nobody cares."

Here's the thing about the bonk: it's overwhelming. It makes the finish line feel impossible. But I've been here before. And because I've faced it so many times, I know its secret. The bonk isn't the end—it's just a test.

When I feel it coming, I don't think about the miles left to run. That's a trap. Thinking about the whole race is like staring at a mountain and trying to climb it in one leap—it's paralyzing. Instead, I get small. I focus on what I can do right now. I ask myself one simple question: "Can I take another step?" That's it. One step. And when I take that step, I ask the question again. Over and over, I keep moving forward, step by step. Each step mirrors the FOGS phases we've journeyed through: starting with a Foundation of mindset to anchor you, building Operations to steady your pace, fueling Growth to push past the pain, and locking in Sustainability to cross the finish line stronger.

Then, something magical happens. As the steps add up, I start to shift my thinking. Instead of dwelling on the pain, I ask myself, "What if?" What if I keep going? What if I'm stronger than I think? What if this ends up being my fastest race? What if I get through this and feel amazing on the other side? Those "what ifs" pull me forward, one hopeful possibility at a time. And eventually, the bonk fades. My rhythm returns, my breath steadies, and I remember why I love running in the first place.

Now, here's where this connects to your business. Because let's be real—every entrepreneur faces their own version of the bonk. Maybe it's a cash flow crisis that keeps you up at night, a project that tanks despite your best efforts, or a competitor who's pulling ahead.

Whatever it is, it feels like the whole world is against you. The voices in your head? They're just as loud. "Why are you even trying? This isn't going to work. You should quit while you're ahead."

The bonk hits everyone—runners, entrepreneurs, you name it. The trick is knowing how to push through. When you expect the obstacles, you don't panic. You don't throw in the towel. You take a breath, assess the situation, and ask yourself the same question I ask on the trail: "Can I take one more step?" Maybe it's calling one more potential client, solving one small problem, or just keeping the doors open for another day. Whatever it is, you take that step. And then another. Small steps build momentum, and momentum creates progress, sustaining your squad through the Gold Phase of FOGS.

What Are Obstacles?

Obstacles in business are like those sneaky hills in a marathon—you know they're coming, but they still hit you harder than expected. They're the things that slow you down, throw you off course, or make you question why you started in the first place. Some obstacles are external, like market shifts or supply chain issues. Others are internal, like poor planning, miscommunication, or plain old burnout. But here's the thing: obstacles aren't roadblocks. They're just hurdles. And with the right mindset and strategies, you can navigate over, around, or straight through them.

Obstacles come in all shapes and sizes, but here are some of the most common one's small business owners run into:

1. Cash Flow Problems

Running out of money—or not having enough to pay the bills on time—is a classic obstacle. Maybe a big client hasn't paid their invoice yet, or unexpected expenses are eating into your budget. Whatever the cause, cash flow issues can make even the most confident business owner feel like the walls are closing in.

2. Time Management Woes

Ever feel like there just aren't enough hours in the day? That's because there aren't. Between managing clients, handling operations, and putting out fires, it's easy to fall into the trap of doing everything yourself and still feeling like nothing's getting done.

3. Customer Complaints

Whether it's a bad review, a demanding client, or a product return, dealing with unhappy customers can derail your focus and your confidence. Worse, it can shake your reputation if it's not handled well.

4. Employee Challenges

Hiring the wrong person, dealing with team drama, or struggling with turnover—your team can either be your greatest asset or a constant headache. If your people aren't aligned or pulling their weight, it feels like you're dragging a wagon uphill.

5. Marketing Misfires

You've spent time and money on an ad campaign, and... crickets. Maybe you're targeting the wrong audience, or maybe your message isn't hitting home. Either way, it's frustrating and expensive.

6. Scaling Pains

Growth sounds great until it happens too fast. Suddenly, you're overwhelmed with orders, your systems can't keep up, and your quality starts to slip. Scaling without a plan is a recipe for chaos.

7. Competition

There's always someone out there trying to do what you do, only faster or cheaper. Keeping up with—or outsmarting—your competitors can feel like a never-ending game of whack-a-mole.

8. Burnout

You're exhausted. You've been pushing so hard for so long that you've forgotten why you started. Burnout isn't just bad for you—it's bad for your business, because you can't lead effectively when you're running on fumes.

Here's the thing: obstacles aren't signs you're doing something wrong. They're proof you're in the game. Every business faces challenges, no matter how big or small. The difference between those who succeed and those who fold is how they handle them. The good news? You've got what it takes to face these hurdles head-on—because if you're reading this, you're already thinking about how to overcome them. And that's the first step.

How to Overcome Obstacles

Overcoming obstacles in business isn't about some magic formula or perfect timing—it's about following a clear, deliberate process. When challenges hit (and they will), here's your step-by-step guide to tackle them head-on:

Step 1: Identify the Obstacle

You can't fix what you don't acknowledge. Start by pinpointing the exact problem. Is it a lack of cash flow, a difficult team member, or a broken process? Be brutally honest about what's going wrong. Ask yourself:

- What's the root cause of this issue?

- How is it impacting my business?

Once you name the obstacle, you've already taken the first step toward overcoming it.

Step 2: Break It Down

Big problems feel paralyzing because we look at them as one giant, unmovable thing. Instead, break it into smaller pieces. Let's say you're losing customers. Break that down:

- Are customers unhappy with your product or service?

- Is your communication falling short?

- Are competitors offering something better?

Breaking the problem into smaller questions gives you clarity and specific areas to address.

Step 3: Assess Your Resources

Before jumping into action, take stock of what you have to work with.

- What skills, tools, or systems do you already have that could help?

- Who on your team can contribute to solving this?

- Do you need outside help or advice?

Sometimes, the answer is already in your toolbox—you just need to step back and see it.

Step 4: Make a Plan

With the problem broken down and your resources identified, it's time to create a plan. But don't overcomplicate it. Keep it simple:

- What's the first step you need to take?

- What's your timeline for fixing this?

- Who's responsible for each part of the solution?

A good plan doesn't just solve the problem; it gets everyone on the same page and moving forward.

Step 5: Take Action

Here's where a lot of people freeze—they get stuck in planning mode. Don't let "perfect" be the enemy of progress. Start small, test your plan, and adapt as you go. Action creates momentum, and momentum is the enemy of obstacles.

Step 6: Monitor and Adjust

As you implement your plan, keep an eye on what's working and what's not. Obstacles rarely have one-and-done solutions. Pay attention to feedback, track your results, and be ready to pivot if something isn't working. This isn't failure—it's part of the process.

Step 7: Stay Consistent

Overcoming obstacles isn't about quick fixes; it's about consistent effort. Whether you're rebuilding a process or repairing a customer relationship, the key is to stick with it. Small, consistent actions lead to big results over time.

Step 8: Learn from the Experience

Once the obstacle is behind you, don't just move on like it never happened. Take a moment to reflect:

- What caused the problem in the first place?
- What worked well in overcoming it?
- What can you do to prevent it from happening again?

Every obstacle is a learning opportunity if you're willing to look for the lesson.

Step 9: Celebrate Your Progress

When you've tackled the obstacle, don't forget to celebrate. Whether it's hitting a milestone, solving a long-standing issue, or just surviving a tough week, recognizing your wins gives you the fuel to face the next challenge with confidence.

Common Pitfalls When Facing Obstacles

Here's the thing about obstacles: they're not just tough—they're tricky. It's easy to stumble into pitfalls that make the challenge feel even harder to overcome. The good news? Most of these pitfalls are avoidable if you know what to look out for. Let's break down the most common traps business owners fall into when dealing with obstacles—and how you can sidestep them like a pro.

1. Ignoring the Problem

- **The Pitfall:** Pretending the obstacle doesn't exist and hoping it'll magically disappear. Spoiler: it won't. Ignoring problems usually makes them worse.

- **The Fix:** Face it head-on. The sooner you acknowledge the issue, the sooner you can start fixing it.

2. Overreacting and Panicking

- **The Pitfall:** Letting stress take over, which leads to rash decisions and half-baked solutions.

- **The Fix:** Take a breath. Stay calm and approach the problem strategically. A clear head is your best tool in a crisis.

3. Blaming Others

- **The Pitfall:** Pointing fingers at employees, customers, or external factors instead of taking responsibility.

- **The Fix:** Own it. Even if the problem wasn't your fault, the solution is your responsibility. Focus on what you can control.

4. Trying to Solve Everything at Once

- **The Pitfall:** Tackling the entire problem as one massive, overwhelming task.

- **The Fix:** Break it down into smaller, manageable steps. Focus on one piece at a time to avoid burnout and confusion.

5. Overcomplicating the Solution

- **The Pitfall:** Creating a solution so elaborate that it's harder to implement than the problem itself.

- **The Fix:** Keep it simple. Focus on practical, actionable steps that get results without unnecessary complexity.

6. Failing to Get Input from Others

- **The Pitfall:** Believing you have to solve the problem alone or refusing to ask for help.

- **The Fix:** Tap into your team, mentors, or peers. Fresh perspectives often lead to better solutions.

7. Giving Up Too Soon

- **The Pitfall:** Throwing in the towel when the first attempt doesn't work.

- **The Fix:** Stay persistent. Adjust your approach, try new tactics, and keep pushing forward. Obstacles take time and effort to overcome.

8. Focusing Only on the Obstacle

- **The Pitfall:** Getting so caught up in the problem that you lose sight of the bigger picture.

- **The Fix:** Step back and ask yourself how this obstacle fits into your long-term goals. This perspective shift can help you see solutions more clearly.

9. Failing to Learn from the Experience

- **The Pitfall:** Solving the problem but not reflecting on what caused it or how to prevent it in the future.

- **The Fix:** Take time to evaluate what worked, what didn't, and what you'll do differently next time.

Sustaining Your Squad with an 85% Retention Metric

In the Gold Phase, sustainability locks in your vision, ensuring the fog never returns. For small team leaders, this means keeping your crew and customers engaged long-term. A key metric to track is customer retention rate, aiming for at least 85%. This measures how many clients stay with you over time—e.g., if you served 100 clients last year and 85 return this year, you've hit 85%. Why 85%? Industry data (per Harvard Business Review, 2024) shows businesses with 80%+ retention see 25% higher profits due to loyal relationships. That's a gold standard your team can aim for.

Case Study: The Gym That Thrived

A 7-person gym team faced a 60% retention rate as members dropped off post-pandemic. The owner set an 85% retention goal, tracking it monthly via their CRM. They assessed feedback—clients wanted varied class options—and adapted by training the team to offer two new weekly sessions. After a 3-month pilot, retention rose to 87%, boosting revenue by 20% as word-of-mouth grew. Their 87% retention came from team training—65% of sustainable businesses invest here, ensuring their team adapts and thrives, just like yours can. The owner celebrated with a team outing, reinforcing squad morale. This metric turned a struggling business into a sustainable powerhouse.

Final Thoughts

Obstacles are an inevitable part of business—they're as certain as taxes and Monday mornings. But they're not the end of the road. They're tests, opportunities, and sometimes even blessings in disguise. The key to overcoming them is your mindset and approach. By recognizing the problem, breaking it down, planning strategically, and avoiding the common pitfalls, you can navigate challenges with confidence and clarity.

Here's the real takeaway: obstacles aren't a sign you're failing. They're a sign you're in the game. They remind you that progress isn't a straight line—it's a winding trail with bumps, detours, and the occasional cliff edge. But if you stay consistent, lean into the process, and trust your ability to adapt, every obstacle becomes a stepping stone to something greater.

So, the next time you hit a roadblock, don't panic. Pause, reassess, and take the next step forward. Because that's all it takes—one step at a time. And before you know it, you'll look back and realize the obstacle that seemed so daunting was just another chapter in your success story. Let's keep moving.

Let's Put This Into Action

A.I. ensures your Sustainability by helping you anticipate challenges before they hit. Tools like QuickBooks with A.I. forecasting can predict cash flow dips based on your spending patterns, giving you months to adjust. A service business might use A.I. to monitor customer churn rates—say, spotting a 10% drop in repeat bookings early, so you can launch a loyalty program to recover. Predictive A.I. keeps your business resilient, not reactive. The A.I. prompt below will help you identify practical solutions to obstacles and forecast risks to plan for a future where the fog stays gone.

Prompt:

"Based on my business data [e.g., revenue trends, expenses], what financial risks might I face in the next 6 months?"

Follow on Prompt:

"I'm facing an obstacle in my business, and I need help overcoming it. The problem is [describe the obstacle in detail, e.g., 'I'm struggling with late payments from clients, which is hurting my cash flow']. My goal is to [state your desired outcome, e.g., 'improve cash flow and reduce late payments']. Can you suggest 5 practical, creative solutions to help me solve this issue, along with steps to implement them?"

A Final Note: Evolving with A.I. for Lasting Sustainability

As your business grows, A.I. will grow with you, keeping you ahead in the Gold Phase of FOGS. Beyond the prompts in this book, explore A.I. tools for deeper insights—like using machine learning to predict market shifts or A.I. chatbots to handle customer inquiries 24/7. A client of mine, a flower shop owner, used A.I. to forecast seasonal demand, stocking up on trending items early and boosting profits by 30%. Another, a consultant, deployed an A.I. chatbot to field routine questions, freeing up 10 hours a week for high-value work. Keep experimenting—A.I. isn't just a tool; it's your partner in building a business that doesn't just survive but dominates for years to come.

☆★☆

Chapter 14:
A LETTER TO YOU

"Dear Reader,

I opened this book with two moments that shaped me—a grueling day in bootcamp, where I stood in formation, sweat-soaked and overwhelmed, every muscle screaming, wondering if I'd ever measure up, and a firefight in Afghanistan, crouched in a dusty valley, the air thick with chaos, gunfire cracking around me, my heart pounding as I tried to lead my squad through a fog so dense I couldn't see the way out. That feeling—the weight of it all, the fear of failing those who depended on me, the sheer exhaustion of pushing forward when everything felt impossible—that's where I started. And I know that's where you were, too, when you first picked up this book. Overwhelmed. Uncertain. Leading your small team through a battlefield of your own, where the fog of business felt just as suffocating as the fog of war I faced.

I see you in that moment. I know the sleepless nights, the endless questions, the pressure of keeping your squad together when the noise of competition, cash flow, and chaos drowns out your clarity. I've been there—on the battlefield and in business—feeling like the ground was slipping beneath me, like no matter how hard I fought, the fog wouldn't lift. I understand the weight you've carried, the doubt that whispers you might not be enough, the exhaustion that makes you wonder if you can keep going. But here's what I also know: you're still here. You've fought through every chapter, every lesson, every hard truth in these pages, and that takes a kind of courage I admire deeply.

You and I, we've walked this journey together. Through these pages, I've watched you cut through the fog of business, just as I learned to lead through the fog of war. We started by finding clarity—building a foundation for your squad that gave you a reason to keep fighting, a north star to guide you when the haze was thickest. Then you sharpened your focus, creating systems to steady your team, turning chaos into order so your crew could march forward as one. You fueled your momentum, growing stronger, taking on bigger challenges, proving to yourself and your squad that you could rise above the noise. And finally, you locked in a legacy, building something that lasts, something your team can carry forward even when the fog tries to creep back in. That's the FOGS journey—Foundation, Operations, Growth, Sustainability—and you've walked it with grit and heart.

I'm proud of you. Not because it was easy—it wasn't—but because you didn't give up. I've felt the same struggles you have, the same doubts, the same bone-deep tiredness that comes from leading through uncertainty. But I've also felt the joy of breaking through, of seeing my team thrive, of knowing I'd built something worth fighting for. You're there now, too. You've turned the fog of business from a wall into a challenge you can conquer. You've learned to lead your squad with clarity and strength, to see through the haze and chart a path forward. And I know you'll keep going, because that's who you are—a leader who doesn't back down, no matter how thick the fog gets.

So as you close this book, take a moment to breathe. Look back at the battlefield you've crossed, the fog you've cut through, the squad you've lifted. The fog of business will always be there, waiting to test you, but now you know how to fight it. You've got the tools, the heart, and the will to lead your team through anything. I believe in you—I've seen what you're capable of, and I know your story is far from over. Keep leading from the front, keep cutting through the fog, and keep building that legacy. Your squad needs you, and I'm rooting for you every step of the way.

With all my respect and belief in you,

Eric McConaty

☆ ☆ ☆

Congratulations! You made it to the finish line—but this is just the beginning.

I've packed this book with ideas and strategies to help you take your business to the next level, but I know there's always more to learn and implement. That's why I've created a hub of free resources, tools, and templates to help you get started right now.

Whether you're looking to build systems, scale smarter, or fine-tune your strategy, you'll find everything you need on my website. These tools are designed to make your journey smoother, faster, and more effective.

Head over to https://tgscoaching.com/resources/ and check out the free resources waiting for you.

Or, just scan the QR code below.

Your business deserves this investment in growth—and you've already taken the first step by finishing this book. Now, let's keep that momentum going. I can't wait to see what you accomplish!

www.ingramcontent.com/pod-product-compliance
Lightning Source LLC
Chambersburg PA
CBHW071546200326
41519CB00021BB/6631